THE HORSE OWNER'S HANDBOOK

THE
HORSE OWNER'S
HANDBOOK

Monty Mortimer

David & Charles

All photographs by the author

© Monty Mortimer 1987

British Library Cataloguing in Publication Data

Mortimer, Monty
   The horse owner's handbook.
   1. Horses
   I. Title
   636.1'083   SF285.3
   ISBN 0-7153-8910-6

First published 1987
Second impression 1989
Third impression 1992

Photoset in Linotron Times by
Northern Phototypesetting Co Bolton
and printed in Great Britain
by Redwood Press Ltd, Melksham, Wilts
for David & Charles
Brunel House   Newton Abbot   Devon

(M) 636. 1083 M

Contents

Introduction

In recent years riding, as a competitive sport or just a relaxing pastime, has grown enormously in popularity. It is no longer the preserve of a privileged few but is enjoyed by a very wide cross-section of the community.

Horses and ponies are kept not only in rural areas but also in urban areas in increasing numbers. Many people who are enjoying the horse today have no background connection with the horse, or any large animal for that matter. Children, even those who live in towns, often develop an interest in riding and want a pony. This can present the 'non-horsy' parents with difficulties when it comes to purchasing, keeping and transporting.

Owning a horse is not unlike being permanently responsible for a new baby. He can do almost nothing for himself, and in the unnatural circumstances in which we keep him he is at risk from many factors.

There is no mystery about good horsemastership; the rules are simple and are largely common sense. To be successful it does however require some study, diligence and a good deal of attention to detail. This book is written for those who are contemplating buying a horse or pony, or who are owners and are looking for some simple guidelines under which they can keep their animals safe, healthy, happy and useful.

1 Buying a Horse

How and Where to Buy

Buying a horse is fraught with dangers and difficulties. It is a hazardous adventure for the experienced horseman and a positive 'minefield' for the inexperienced.

Deciding upon the type of horse that is required is probably the first hurdle to overcome. Whilst it is a pleasure to own, and flattering to be seen riding a young, chestnut thoroughbred, such a horse may not be temperamentally suited to the novice rider. To buy a novice three-year-old pony for a novice child in the hope that they will learn and grow up together is usually a recipe for disaster. Novice horses are best with experienced riders and novice riders are better off with correctly trained horses of some experience on which they can learn.

Before buying the following points should be considered:

1 What breed is preferred?
2 What height should it be?
3 What weight has it to carry?
4 Is it to be a hunter or a competition horse, eg in show jumping, dressage, gymkhanas, Pony Club events, long distance riding etc?
5 Has it to live in or out?
6 How much time can be spent riding and looking after the horse?
7 Has it to be good in traffic?
8 Has it to be clipped, boxed or shod?
9 Has it to be unblemished or a straight mover?
10 What funds are available?

When these questions are answered there are, broadly, three ways in which a horse can be purchased: from an auction sale; from a dealer; privately.

If the horse is purchased at a sale there are 'conditions of sale' listed in the catalogue designed to protect the purchaser and the vendor. Most auctions are scrupulously fair and honest. The auctioneers have these conditions of sale drawn up by their legal advisers to ensure that both parties receive a fair deal. It is imperative that the purchaser reads and understands these conditions before bidding for a horse at a sale.

Each horse is described in the catalogue in full. He may be listed as 'A good hunter, quiet in traffic and to box and shoe'. What is *not* said in the catalogue is probably more important than what *is* said. This horse may be difficult, if not impossible, to clip. If a horse bought at a sale does not conform in every way with the catalogue description there is usually a proviso that he may be returned to the vendor within forty-eight hours of purchase and a full refund of the purchase price made. This would be very unpopular with the vendor, who will still be liable to pay the auctioneer's commission.

Horses bought at a sale should be examined by a veterinary surgeon either before or immediately after purchase. A veterinary surgeon will issue, for a fee, a certificate which, though not a guarantee, is a certified professional opinion.

Some auction sales provide facilities for prospective purchasers or their assistants/advisers to ride and jump horses in which they are interested. It is usually sensible to ask the vendor to ride the horse first. Should he decline to do so it may be interesting to find out why. An inexperienced purchaser would do well to take an experienced horseman with him.

No guarantee can be given that a horse is absolutely sound. A cursory examination only can be given but this is usually an adequate guide. A thorough examination requires extensive, technical tests which are costly and usually unnecessary. They would be made on only the most expensive horses.

It is sensible to ask the vendor some detailed and searching questions, for example:

1 Do you guarantee that the horse is a good hunter?
2 Do you guarantee that he is quiet in traffic?
3 Do you guarantee that he has no stable tricks or vices?
4 Do you guarantee that he is not on drugs of any sort?
5 Why are you selling him?

There is no guide to the price of horses as there is for motor cars. Prices vary with the current state of the market, the time of year and from county to county, and will depend on:

1 Age. Very young or very old horses will command a lower price than the mature horse at, or coming up to, his prime.
2 Pedigree. Horses by a sire whose progeny have proved themselves in a particular way may command a higher price than those of doubtful ancestry.
3 Blemishes. Capped hocks or elbows, old wounds or signs of wear and tear (puffy joints, wind galls, thickened tendons etc) will all detract from the price.

One major disadvantage of buying a horse at a sale is that the purchase price will be subject to Value Added Tax.

A plain horse may not command the same price as a handsome one but there is a true saying in the horse world, 'handsome is as handsome does' which means that it does not matter what he looks like if he is honest, sound and does a good job. It may be necessary when buying a horse to accept a few blemishes to be able to stay within one's budget.

Unsoundness must be avoided as it will only lead to disappointment. Vices, both in the stable and when the horse is being ridden, are usually the result of bad or incorrect training. They may, in time, be corrected by an expert but there is no guarantee that they will not return. They are best avoided by the novice purchaser.

Buying a horse from a reputable dealer is often a satisfactory course. There are many honest dealers in spite of the well established folklore that surrounds this profession. No dealer who values his reputation will sell a client an unsuitable horse. Horses that behave badly in public quickly draw attention to themselves and word soon gets around as to their origin. Should a horse prove to be unsuitable, the dealer will almost certainly take it back and provide another, usually with some cash adjustment in his favour. Again, a disadvantage in buying a horse from a dealer is that the price will almost certainly include VAT.

Without doubt the most satisfactory way to buy a horse is to find one that is recommended by a friend, or that one knows. A private purchase is hardly likely to be subject to VAT and there is a greater possibility of giving the horse a thorough trial. There is even the possibility of having the horse on trial for a short period. The potential dangers and difficulties are, however, obvious.

Leasing a horse is a possible alternative to buying. A clear contract should be drawn up in writing between both the lessor and lessee which should be approved by a solicitor. Borrowing a horse or pony is a risky practice and should be avoided.

Types and Breeds of Horses and Ponies

There are many breeds, crossbreeds and types from which to choose a riding horse, and good and bad horses in each variety. Individual breeds have their own characteristics which make them more suitable or less suitable for various equestrian activities. The British Isles are particularly rich in indigenous breeds and those that have, over the years, become established as native.

The wealth of native pony breeds, nine in all, provides an excellent choice of pure breds and crosses. The English thoroughbred is the backbone of performance horse breeding. Other British horses, the Cleveland Bay and the various heavy horses, all contribute to the provision of a choice that is unrivalled in any other country.

Native ponies

Connemara   This pony originated in western Ireland and is now successfully bred in Britain and elsewhere. The predominant colour is grey, but it may also be dun, black, bay, chestnut or roan; never piebald or skewbald. Heights range from 13 to 14.2 hands, making it a useful competition pony for children and adults in many disciplines. It is a hardy, bold, good-tempered pony with good action. It should have a fine head, sloping shoulder and good bone. The Connemara is used extensively in the production of very good crossbreeds.

Dales   The Dales is bred in the north of England and is a hardy pony, 14 to 14.2 hands, capable of carrying and pulling heavy loads. It is usually black with a long flowing mane and tail, and long silky hair on the lower legs and heels. It should be a free mover, with a short, strong back, well laid shoulder and good bone. The Dales/thoroughbred cross has been known to make a useful pony for many types of riding.

Dartmoor   This is an excellent children's pony, often making a very good show pony when crossed with the Arab. It must not exceed 12.2 hands and must have a small head and tiny ears. Black, bay and brown are the usual colours, but never piebald or skewbald.

Exmoor   This pony comes from north Devon and Somerset. It is slightly stronger and bigger than the Dartmoor, excellent for children and good in harness. Mares should not exceed 12.2 hands, stallions 12.3 hands. Exmoors are bay or brown and easily recognised by their 'mealy' or oatmeal-coloured muzzles. The coat is harsh and springy in winter but close and shining in summer.

Fell   Native to the north of England, this is a strong, hardy, sure-footed pony. Height ranges from 13.2 to 14 hands, making the Fell a useful hunting and trekking pony for adults and children. It is good in harness and as a mount for the disabled. Colour can be black, brown, bay or grey.

Highland   A strong, active but docile pony which originated in the Highlands and Western Isles of Scotland. It can be from 13 to 14.2 hands, making a good all-round pony for children and adults. It is intelligent, easily trained and makes a good jumper.

New Forest   A good family pony with an upper limit of 14.2 hands. Docile and easy to train, the New Forest pony is successful in the Pony Club and in jumping and working classes. The larger ponies have more substance and are suited to adults whilst remaining narrow enough for children. They come in all colours except piebald, skewbald and blue-eyed cream.

Shetland   This is the smallest of the native breeds. The Shetland's height does not exceed 42in at maturity which, with its intelligence and docile nature, makes it an ideal pony for the smallest children. It can take part in all types of riding competitions for small ponies. All colours and mixtures are found.

Welsh Cob/Pony   This breed is divided into four groups: A, B, C and D. All these groups have common characteristics: an attractive head, broad dished forehead, bold eyes, small ears, rounded jowl and flared nostrils. These ponies have a strong presence and very elegant movement.

In Section A, the pony must not exceed 12 hands in height. Its intelligence and gentle nature make it an ideal leading-rein pony or child's first pony. It is crossed successfully with the thoroughbred and riding ponies. Mainly grey, but all colours are accepted except piebald and skewbald. Blue eyes are not uncommon.

Section B is a larger version of Section A but not exceeding 13.2 hands in height. It is an ideal child's second pony.

Section C is a stronger version of the Welsh pony. Not exceeding 13.2 hands it usually has an element of Welsh cob in its blood. Its increased strength makes it a good pony for adults. Like all the Welsh ponies it is a naturally good mover and jumper and makes a good harness pony.

Section D, the Welsh cob, has no height limit; it can reach 16 hands and is therefore not strictly a pony. It is an elegant mover, good jumper and works well in harness. This pony is known for its great presence, panache and courage.

Horses

English throughbred This is probably the world's best known horse and is now found in almost every country. The breed was started in England during the latter half of the seventeenth and the first half of the eighteenth centuries when three Arab stallions were imported: the Byerley Turk in 1689, the Darley Arabian in 1704 and the Godolphin Arabian in 1730. These stallions formed the basic breeding sires and all thoroughbred horses can trace their ancestry to one of the three. They are horses of great beauty and courage, particularly fast and with great stamina. One of their main attributes is the ability to pass on these great qualities, with a high degree of reliability, to their progeny. Thoroughbred horses may be any colour, but roans and multi-colours are unlikely, and the height can be from 14.3 hands up to 16.2 hands or more. All thoroughbred horses are registered in the General Stud Book and only registered horses may race under Jockey Club rules.

It is not only in racing that the thoroughbred is so outstanding.

Hunting, polo, dressage, horse trials, show jumping and showing are all areas in which the thoroughbred or its influence can be found. It is not entirely suitable for all types of riding, however, and its high courage and temperament are not ideal for modern high-level dressage, although thoroughbreds are sometimes found performing well at the highest level. Their legs are not always capable of withstanding the rough and tumble of cross country riding and jumping, and many thoroughbred horses, that are superb performers in every other way, have difficulty in staying sound. As a general rule the thoroughbred is not a suitable mount for a beginner or a novice rider.

The thoroughbred horse is used extensively as a cross with almost every other breed to add the best of its qualities to theirs. Regrettably, many top quality horses have been exported, which has meant the loss of an irrecoverable aspect of the national heritage and has allowed the breeding of low grade, so-called 'thoroughbreds' over which the nation has no control.

Cob   The cob is not a breed but a type. It is so popular as a riding horse that its characteristics are well known and cob classes are held at most major shows. It is big-bodied, short-legged with strong quarters and gaskins. The cannons should be very short and strong, the back short and the girth large. The cob is a placid, docile horse making an excellent choice of hunter for the nervous, or those who are not so agile. The height is unlikely to exceed 15.2 hands.

Arab   This very ancient breed has, over the years, had a major influence on many other breeds. It is a horse of great beauty, usually having a silky coat and a full, flowing mane and tail. The Arab has great courage and intelligence, and is particularly known for its stamina – equestrian history tells many stories of its great feats of endurance. In present-day competition it is a favourite of those who take part in long distance riding contests.

The breed was originally chestnut or bay, and chestnut is generally preferred; they are sometimes white or grey, and black is rare. The accepted height limits are 14.2 to 15 hands, although the modern Arab horse is sometimes a little over 15 hands high.

Cleveland Bay   As the name implies, this is always a bay horse

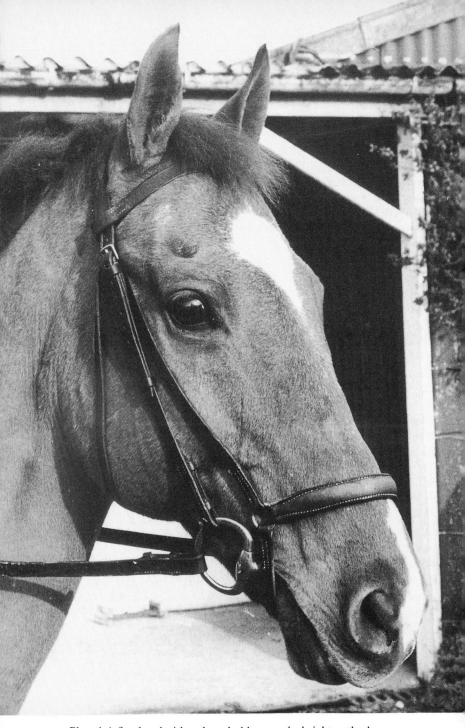

Plate 1 A fine head with a clear, bold eye and a bright outlook

and it is claimed to be the oldest of the British native breeds. It is a particular favourite in North Yorkshire and South Durham, the Cleveland area from which it comes. The average height for this breed is 15.3 to 16 hands. It has a large body, short legs and a large head with long ears on a long thin neck. The shoulder and pastern tend to be upright. Whilst this description does not conjure up an elegant image, the Cleveland Bay is a powerful horse of a beautiful rich bay. Its conformation, strength and colour consistency make it an excellent carriage horse, especially where matched teams are required.

Other breeds There are many other breeds and types of horse, including the exotics from eastern Europe, Asia and the Orient. More and more European breeds – the Holstein, Hanoverian, Trakehner, Dutch, Swedish, Irish Draught and other 'warm bloods' – are found in their pure form or as crosses bringing their individual qualities to the riding horses that are available at sales and on the open market.

The Conformation of the Horse

It is not possible to learn how to assess a horse's conformation from a textbook. One can develop an 'eye for a horse' only by looking at and studying as many different types as possible. Horses come in all shapes and sizes and it is this variety that makes the horse so eminently suitable for so many different types of work.

The various strengths and weaknesses that most horses possess make them more or less suitable for various tasks. Some weaknesses would not be tolerated for some disciplines. A heavy, short-legged horse would clearly not be suitable to train for the Derby but may make an excellent hunter for an elderly, heavyweight gentleman. Likewise, the horse that has all the attributes and physical requirements of a Derby winner would almost certainly not be suitable for the riding school. There are, however, certain physical features that apply to all types of horse. These will either add to or detract from their ability to be trained in any riding discipline.

The first, and most important, aspect is that the horse should appear to be all one animal. His head should not be obviously too big or too small for his body. His neck should not be too long and thin or too short and thick. His legs should not appear to be too long or too short. Generally, he should give a well balanced appearance, whatever his type or breed.

The head should be fine with a clear, large, bright eye. Small eyes are sometimes a sign of bad temper. Good breadth between the eyes gives good peripheral vision. The nostrils should be large, giving plenty of room for inhaling air. The head should be well set onto the neck and neither too thick nor too thin through the gullet. A horse that is too thick through the gullet may have some difficulty with the head carriage. The result of this may be some restriction in breathing when the neck is raised and arched and the horse flexes at the poll. If he is too thin through the gullet it may also create difficulties with the head carriage and restrict the passage of air to the lungs and food to the stomach. The ears should be correct for that particular horse, neither too big nor too small. 'Lop' ears are a matter of personal choice but do sometimes denote a quiet and generous horse.

The neck is a very important part of the horse. It carries his head, which is large and heavy, and is used to help him keep his balance. The free nodding of the head in rhythm with the stride in walk, canter and gallop is vital if the horse is to use himself efficiently. A strong neck enables the horse to carry his head correctly. The 'ewe' neck (the thin neck that appears to curve upwards) is a sign of weakness in the horse and like the short, thick, heavy neck may detract from his ability to be trained correctly. The neck should be well set into the body, neither too high nor too low. Some dressage trainers have a preference for the horse with a neck that comes fairly upright from the withers as this is the position that they would try to achieve in the advanced horse. Trainers in other disciplines may find that the horse with similar conformation of the neck is difficult to train.

The shoulder should be long and with a good slope. The horse with upright shoulders may be an uncomfortable ride and may be prone to concussion problems in the forelegs and feet. An upright shoulder may also restrict the swing of the forelegs, making the lengthening of the steps difficult.

The width of the breast between the forelegs should be good to allow plenty of heart and lung room in the rib-cage, and also to allow unrestricted movement of the forelegs. The barrel should be full and round with the ribs well sprung. This again gives plenty of room for the heart and lungs and helps with the horse's respiration.

The back should be short, flat and strong. It is a most important part of the riding horse and is subjected to a good deal of wear and tear. Whilst some mares have long backs to enable them to carry the foal, a long back is often a sign of weakness. The loins should be round, strong and well muscled. The quarters, too, should be full, round and well muscled. They are the 'power house' of the horse where most of his driving force is developed.

In the foreleg, the forearm should be long and well muscled. The knee should be large, flat and near the ground. It can be an advantage for the horse to be a little 'over' at the knee as this tends to take the strain off the back tendons when jumping or galloping. The horse should never be 'back' at the knee as this puts strain on the back tendons and the knee joint, particularly when jumping. The cannon bone should be short and thick. It is measured in circumference just below the knee, including the tendons, which is the measurement referred to when a horse is described as having 'eight and a half inches of bone'.

A long sloping pastern, parallel to the slope of the shoulder will give a comfortable ride and relieve some of the concussion to the feet and legs. A very long, sloping pastern will, however, put strain on the back tendons. The short, upright pastern tends to accompany boxy feet and contracted heels. This conformation usually increases the adverse effects of concussion on the limbs. Either extreme is undesirable.

In the hind leg the distance from the hip to the hock should be long with a good slope. The gaskin, or second thigh as it is sometimes called, should be round and well developed. The hock joint, like the knee, should be big, flat and near the ground. It is a vital joint and any weakness here may well detract from the usefulness of the horse. Straight, sickle or 'cow' hocks are all weaknesses that should be avoided. The cannon (or shannon bone in the hind leg) should be short, thick and strong. The back tendons in both the fore and hind legs should be hard, cold and straight, with no signs of bowing or enlargement.

Both hind feet and forefeet should be the right size for the horse. The slope of the foot should be a continuation of the slope of the pastern bone. The sole should be hard and healthy, the frog well formed and springy. Upright or 'boxy' feet with

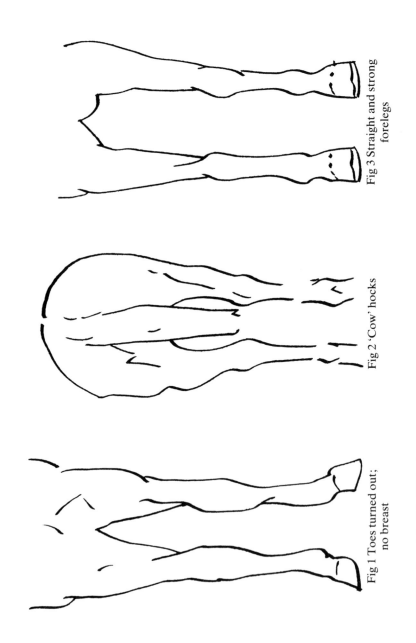

Fig 1 Toes turned out; no breast

Fig 2 'Cow' hocks

Fig 3 Straight and strong forelegs

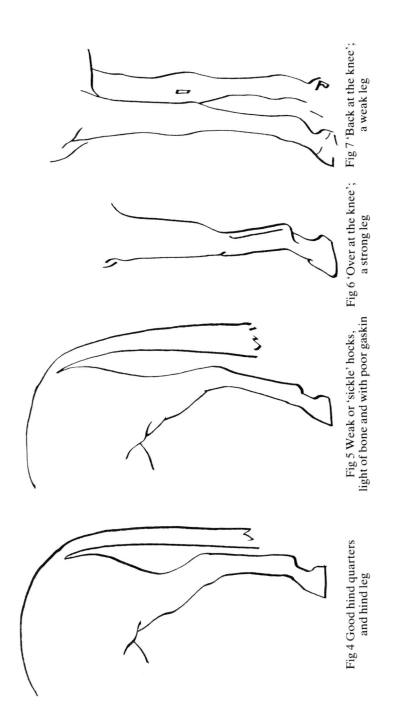

Fig 4 Good hind quarters
and hind leg

Fig 5 Weak or 'sickle' hocks,
light of bone and with poor gaskin

Fig 6 'Over at the knee';
a strong leg

Fig 7 'Back at the knee';
a weak leg

contracted heels are prone to navicular disease and other problems caused by concussion in the foot.

The tail should be well set on, neither too high nor too low, but the set varies to some extent in different breeds of horse. The carriage of the tail is often an indication of the horse's well-being and temperament.

Measuring the height of the horse
The height of the horse is measured in 'hands', one hand being 4in. Where the horse is not a complete number of hands the fractions are measured in inches. The horse may therefore be '15 hands and 2in high'. He should be measured unshod, standing naturally on hard, level ground, with his head at a natural level. His height is the vertical distance from the highest part of the withers to the ground (see Fig 9).

Fig 8 Measuring the height of the horse

Colours and Markings

For the purposes of identification and registration it is necessary to be able to describe horses by their colour and their facial and leg markings. There is a widely understood and accepted system for describing such characteristics.

Bay This colour can range from very light tan through all the shades of brown to a dark mahogany, but the 'points' (muzzle, mane, tail and extremities of the legs) must be black.

Brown Distinctly brown in colour, including the points.

Black Distinctly black all over.

Chestnut Can vary from a light golden colour to dark liver chestnut. The points are a similar chestnut.

Grey Can mean any shade from pure white to dark iron grey. The dapple grey has a very attractive dark and light mottled appearance. A 'flea-bitten' grey is white with small darker grey flecks giving a rather flea-bitten appearance. Grey horses tend to get whiter as they age and flea-bitten greys are usually older.

Roan There are two classes: the 'red' or 'strawberry', and 'blue'; the appearance of the coat is produced by the intermingling of red, white and yellow, or black, white and yellow hairs respectively. The red roan is sometimes called 'sorrel' and occasionally a chestnut roan may be met.

Piebald White and black in large random patches.

Skewbald White and any other colour or colours, usually in large, random patches.

Dun A fawn, biscuit colour, usually with black points.

Colour is sometimes an indication of a horse's temperament. The question is however surrounded by legend and old wives' tales. Bright chestnuts, for instance, have a reputation for being fiery and dark bays are said to be sensible and reliable, but many exceptions could be found to refute these theories. A strong colour is often the sign of a strong horse whether it is a good rich bay or brown or a deep liver chestnut. Weak colours, a washy chestnut or a pale bay with mealy-coloured legs, may well be a sign of a weak horse.

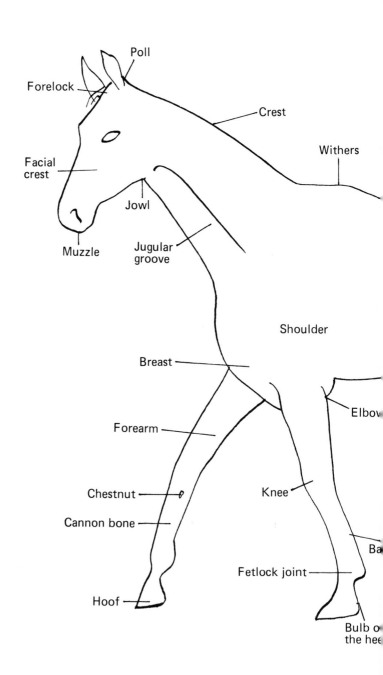

Poll

Forelock

Crest

Withers

Facial
crest

Jowl

Muzzle

Jugular
groove

Shoulder

Breast

Elbow

Forearm

Chestnut

Knee

Ba

Cannon bone

Fetlock joint

Hoof

Bulb o
the hee

Fig 9 The points of the horse

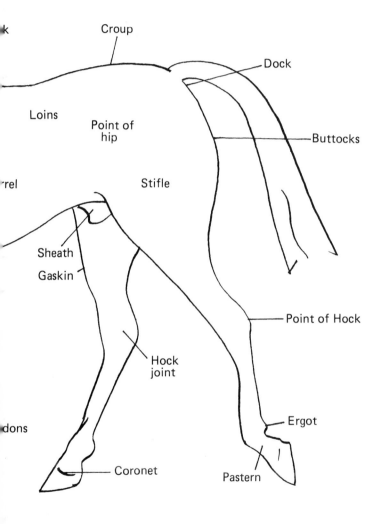

k

Croup

Dock

Loins

Point of
hip

Buttocks

rel

Stifle

Sheath

Gaskin

Point of Hock

Hock
joint

dons

Ergot

Coronet

Pastern

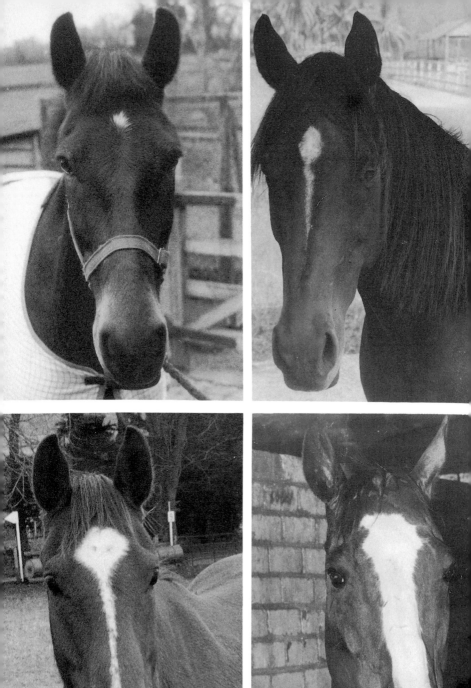

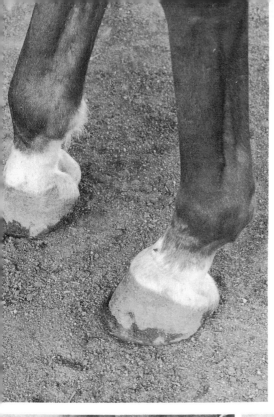

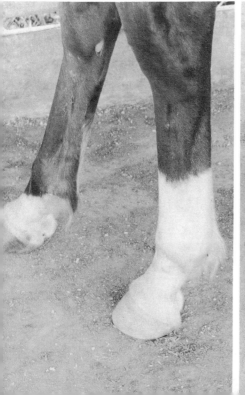

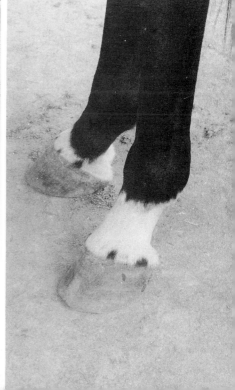

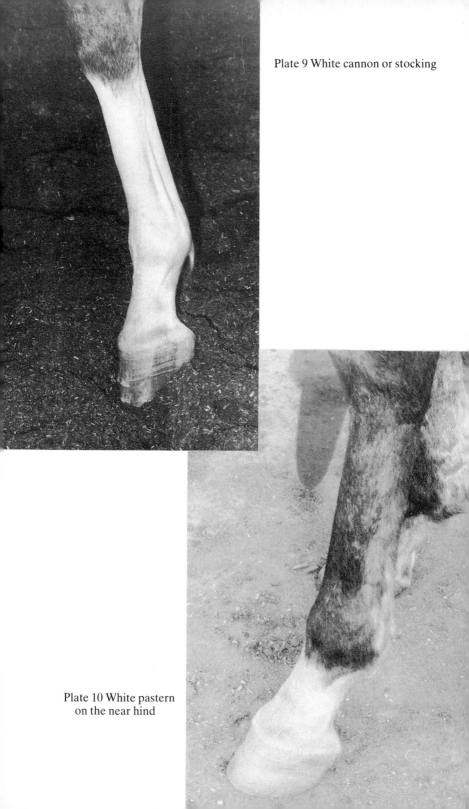

Plate 9 White cannon or stocking

Plate 10 White pastern
on the near hind

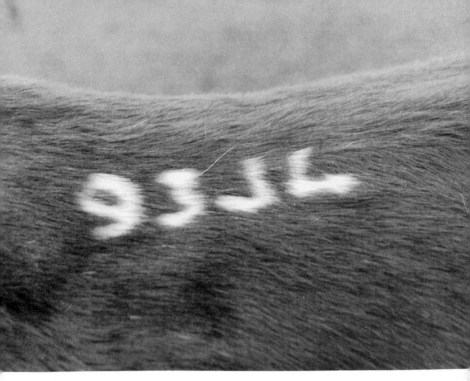

Plate 11 A freeze-marked registered number showing in a long winter coat

Many horses have white facial markings, as illustrated in Plates 2–5. White markings on the legs are also common. These are illustrated in Plates 6–10.

Other markings are sometimes found on the horse's body. The black stripe that runs along the back of some horses from the mane to the tail, often found on the dun horse or pony, is known as the 'dorsal stripe', the 'list' or the 'ray'. The horizontal stripes sometimes found on the legs are known as 'zebra marks'.

The horse's eyes are usually black but where the eye is blue or greyish-white it is known as a wall eye.

Horses are sometimes identified by 'freeze-marking', ie a type of branding where the horse's coat is permanently marked with a white registered number. This is a particularly useful form of identification as it will, in most cases, deter a thief.

Assessing the Age of the Horse

An ability to assess accurately the age of a horse is a skill that the horse owner should develop. It is particularly useful when buying or selling horses.

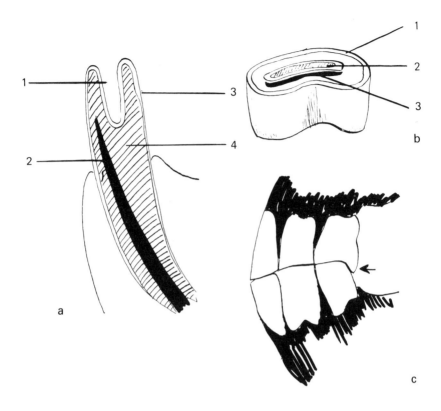

a

b

c

Fig 10a A section through the horse's tooth showing: 1 the infundibulum; 2 the fang hole; 3 the enamel; 4 the dentin

Fig 10b The table of the tooth showing: 1 the enamel; 2 the mark; 3 the dental star

Fig 10c The horse's incisor teeth showing the 'seven year hook' in the corner tooth of the upper jaw

Fig 10d The five-year-old mouth. The tush has erupted and is still fairly sharp; it will round with age. The centrals and laterals are in wear but the corners show little change as yet

Fig 10e The five-year-old mouth in profile. Compare this with Fig 10f; the corner teeth are still rounded

Fig 10f This view of the six-year-old mouth shows the grinding surfaces of the corner teeth worn flat

Fig 10g At ten years the teeth are beginning to lengthen and the tables become more triangular. The mark begins to recede to the back of the table

Fig 10h At fifteen years the teeth are becoming longer and the slope increases. Galvayne's groove is about half way down the corner tooth

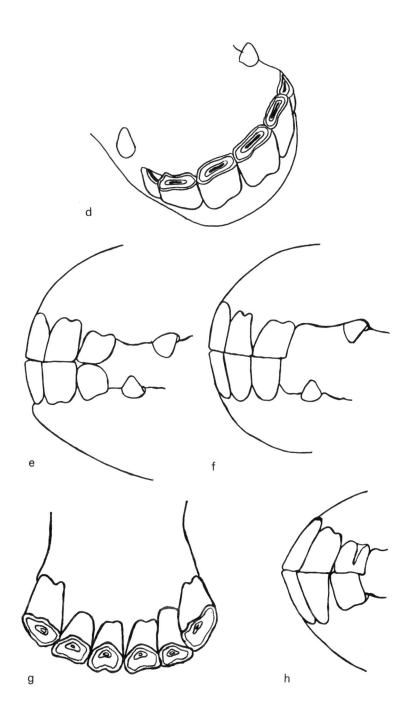

d

e

f

g

h

Whilst it is easy to identify the young horse by his bright, youthful appearance, rounded shape, absence of signs of wear and tear, and bright clear eye, or the older horse by his more angular appearance, puffy joints, sunken cavity above the eye, dipped back, grey hairs etc, it is not so easy to tell the age accurately without close examination of the teeth.

Unlike human teeth, the horse's teeth continue to grow throughout his life, and as he masticates his food they are continually worn down. It is these two factors that enable the horse's age to be assessed by the examination of the teeth.

The horse has between 36 and 44 teeth arranged in three groups: molar or cheek teeth of which there are 24, 6 in the upper jaw on each side and 6 in the lower jaw on each side; 4 canine teeth which appear in the male and sometimes in mares, at maturity, one on each side of the upper and lower jaws; and the incisors, which are in the front of the mouth, 6 on the upper and 6 on the lower jaw. It is the wear of these incisors which shows the horse's age. The two incisor teeth in the middle of the six are called the 'centrals'. Those on either side of the centrals are called the 'laterals' and on either side of the laterals are the 'corner' teeth.

To be able to assess the age of the horse it is necessary to understand the structure of the individual teeth. Fig 10c shows a section through an incisor tooth. The part above the jaw is called the 'crown' and the part within the jaw is the 'fang'. The tooth is made of dentine, a dense tissue which is covered in enamel. The dip in the top of the tooth, which becomes filled with masticated food, is called the 'infundibulum'. This appears on the top surface of the tooth (the 'table') as a brownish patch. As the tooth is worn down this 'mark', as it is known, becomes smaller. At about eight years of age the tip of the fang hole appears on the table of the tooth as a black strip just in front of the mark. This is known as the 'dental star'.

At birth, or very soon after, the foal will have two central, temporary incisor teeth in the upper and lower jaws. At six months, or thereabouts, the temporary lateral teeth will appear and at one year old he will have grown his temporary corner teeth. At one year old the centrals and the laterals will be well in wear but the corners, as yet, will hardly be touching and will show very little wear. At two years of age all the temporary incisor teeth will be in wear. At this age it is possible to mistake the two-year-old mouth for a five-year-old unless one is able to tell temporary from permanent teeth.

The temporary tooth is small, white and shell-like in appearance, with a distinct neck. The permanent tooth is more yellow in colour, being bigger and stronger. As the horse ages the teeth become long with a distinct slope. The tables of the teeth in older horses are oval at first but become more triangular in shape as time passes.

At two years, therefore, the horse has a full set of temporary incisor teeth that are all in wear. At two and a half years of age the permanent central teeth appear and the temporary centrals are pushed out. At three the permanent centrals are in wear. At three and a half years the permanent laterals appear and the temporary laterals are pushed out. At four the permanent laterals are in wear. At four and a half the permanent corners appear and the temporary corners are pushed out. At five the horse has a 'full mouth'. At six all the permanent teeth are in wear. At seven years of age a hook appears on the corner teeth of the upper jaw where the posterior corners of the bottom teeth have worn into them.

By eight years of age the mark is worn well down and the tip of the fang hole is beginning to show in front of it. The tables will be more triangular, the teeth more sloping and becoming longer. At nine to ten years of age a brown groove usually begins to appear at the top of the upper corner teeth in roughly the middle of each tooth. This is known as 'Galvayne's groove'. It grows to about half-way down the tooth at fifteen years, to the bottom at twenty, half-way out by twenty-five and grows out all together at about thirty.

These guidelines should be applied with care and intelligence. There are many factors that can affect the horse's teeth and which may mislead one when trying to assess the horse's age. The diet may affect the wear on the teeth, and a crib biter may damage his teeth. A horse over ten years old is said to be 'aged' as it is difficult to make an accurate assessment with any degree of certainty.

2 The Stabled and the Grass-kept Horse

Stables and Buildings
The horse is perfectly well suited to live in his natural environment on a grassy plain. He needs shelter from the wind and rain, grass and clean water. Living under these conditions, however, he will be able to do only a little light work.

If he is to be employed as a riding horse, with perhaps the demands of competition work being put upon him, he then needs to be kept in a controlled environment, ie in a stable where he can be kept warm and dry and his diet can be regulated. Whilst living out he will grow fat and a long coat to protect him from the elements. Neither of these will allow him to be used seriously in hard work.

The competition horse, or hunter, if he is to do really well, must therefore be kept in. A loose box is the most suitable form of stabling and this must provide:

1 Warmth and protection from the elements.
2 Fresh air but no draughts.
3 Good drainage and dry standing.
4 Good light, by day and night.
5 A constant water supply.
6 Facilities for feeding.
7 Sufficient room to move around, lie down and stand up easily.
8 Security from thieves and vandals.

Careful selection of the site on which stables are to be built is essential. Whilst other planning considerations will effect the choice there are some fundamental factors that should be seriously considered.

A south-facing site with protection from the prevailing winds is the ideal. The top of a windy hill or the bottom of a damp frost hollow should be avoided. Ease of maintenance must be taken into account. If the stables are near to the owner's dwelling the advantages are obvious: ease of access and observation, more economical provision of access roads, water mains and electricity. The layout of the site must allow for the daily running of the stable yard to be carried out quickly and efficiently. The tack room, feed room and stable should be close together to avoid carrying saddles and feeds over long distances. A well-lit, covered way between these buildings is an advantage in wet weather or on dark winter evenings.

A hay and bedding store is required, large enough to allow stocks to be purchased economically. This will depend on the number of horses being fed but it is helpful to be able to buy and store as much as possible at the time of year when hay and straw are at their cheapest – hay in June or July, straight off the field, and straw at harvest time. Again, the barn or store for bulk stocks should be close enough to avoid carrying heavy loads over long distances.

Should space permit, the following facilities will assist in the smooth running of a stable yard:

1 A well-lit area with a hard standing in which the blacksmith can work.
2 Adequate car and box or trailer parking area.
3 A place for drying wet rugs, tack, bandages etc.
4 Lavatory and washing facilities.

The access road should be suitable for lorries to carry heavy loads of forage and bedding as near as possible to the store in which they are to be kept. The whole yard area should be as secure as possible to deter thieves and to prevent horses getting out onto the roads.

The loose box
Many stables are built of wood, often being prefabricated by a contractor and assembled on a concrete base on site. They offer a wide choice of sizes and styles together with integrated ancillary buildings such as tack rooms, feed rooms, etc.

The advantages of wooden stables are that they are reasonably priced, quickly assembled and pleasing to look at. The disadvantages are the fire risk, problems of maintenance, lack of warmth and shorter life-span than that of brick or stone. Also, horses tend to chew woodwork. Stables made of brick, stone or concrete blocks are more permanent constructions. They are less of a fire risk and provide greater warmth. The cost will almost certainly be greater than building in wood.

To accomodate a horse of 16 hands high or over, a loose box measuring 3.65 × 3.65m (12 × 12ft) is required. For horses under 16 hands, 3.65 × 3m (12 × 10ft) may be acceptable, depending on the type of horse and the design of the box. Boxes that measure 3 × 3m (10 × 10ft) are really only suitable, as permanent accommodation, for ponies. Loose boxes measuring 3.65 × 4.3m (12 × 14ft) or even 4.3 × 4.3m (14 × 14ft) are sometimes found. These are suitable for foaling boxes or for very large horses. They require more bedding which results in greater expenditure and more work mucking out.

The stable door is best if it is divided so that the top half can be left open. Its overall height should not be less than 2.15m (7ft). The bottom half of the door should be about 1.4–1.5m (4½–5ft) in height. The width of the door should not be less than 1.2m (4ft). Both halves of the door must be fitted with bolts, top and bottom, on the outside. A kick bolt can be used for the bottom of the door to avoid constant bending down.

The window should be on the same side of the box as the door to avoid draughts. Stable windows are best hinged at the bottom and opening inwards. They should be sited as high as possible in the box and protected by a metal grille so that the horse can not come into contact with the glass.

To enable the horse to be tied up, a metal ring must be securely fitted to the wall. This should be about 1.7m (5½ft) from the ground. Another ring at a similar height is useful for hanging a hay net.

Both internal and external lights are needed. The external light must be of the approved weatherproof variety. The internal light is best sited in the middle of the ceiling; it must be fireproof and inaccessible to the horse. A 150 watt bulb is a suitable size in the average loose box. The switches for both lights must be of weatherproof design and fitted to the outside of the loose box out of reach of the horse.

The floor of the box must provide a dry, non-slip, hard standing. Many old stable floors are built from blue or buff stable bricks or tiles. These are excellent but expensive and require a lot of work to keep them free from compacted stable manure. Modern stable floors are usually made of concrete, which must be durable, non-absorbent and waterproof. Contractors laying these floors should be conversant with the various reports prepared on the subject by the Cement Marketing Company Ltd. To save work and bedding, good drainage is essential. The stable floor should be well sloped; a drop of 4.5cm (1½–2in) in 3m (10ft) provides adequate drainage and will not cause discomfort to the horse.

The overall drainage must also be carefully considered. Besides the foul water drainage from inside the box, the evacuation of rain water from the roofs of the stables and other buildings is very important if the stable yard is to remain serviceable throughout the year.

The ceiling of a loose box should be at least 3m (10ft) high. Adequate thermal insulation should be laid between the ceiling and the roof. The material from which the ceiling is made should be capable of withstanding acid and humid conditions, easy to clean and finished in a light colour. A glossy surface should be avoided as it encourages condensation and the eventual dripping of water into the box.

Plate 12 A corner manger; inexpensive, functional and easy to clean

Facilities for feeding and watering must be provided in each box. Short feed is usually given in a manger which is a large bowl made of either galvanised iron or strong plastic. The manger should be fitted into a strong permanent stand preferably made of brick or stone; the top should be about 1m (3ft) above the ground. Mangers made of glazed pottery are sometimes found in older stables; these are satisfactory apart from the fact that they are permanent fixtures and cannot be removed for cleaning.

Hay is fed either from a hay net fastened to a ring in the wall or in a hay rack. The fitting of the rack is a matter of choice. It can be at a height of about 1.5m (5ft), where it is safe and easy to fill, or at about 1m (3ft) high, where it is less safe but enables the horse to eat at a more natural height.

Water can be supplied in buckets, which should be properly secured, or in an automatic drinker which the horse learns to operate by pressing with his nose. Whichever system is used it must ensure a regular supply of fresh, cold water. All pipes and equipment must be adequately lagged to prevent the water from freezing.

Plate 13 The automatic drinker

The tack room

This must be large enough to enable all the saddles, bridles and other tack to be hung up tidily. The room must be well lit and dry. To ensure that the tack is kept in good condition a constant room temperature must be maintained. A ½Kw tube heater is ideal, as it is both adequate and safe. Heaters that burn gas or oil are unsuitable as they are a potential fire hazard and create condensation.

A sink with hot and cold running water is required for washing and cleaning. A wooden saddle horse is needed for cleaning saddles, together with a large hook hung from the ceiling for cleaning bridles. Adequate storage cupboards for rugs, spare tack, travelling equipment etc are an advantage. An electric power point will also be found useful. The tack room is usually a convenient place to keep the veterinary first-aid cabinet.

Saddlery is expensive equipment for which there is usually a flourishing second-hand market. This makes saddlery theft very rewarding, so a major aspect of the tack room should be that it is burglar proof.

The feed room

This room must be large enough to enable economical stocks of food to be stored. Cereals such as oats, barley and maize must be kept in vermin-proof, preferably galvanised iron, containers. If they are kept in bags they deteriorate quickly and attract rats and mice. Sufficient space should be available for the preparation of feeds, equipment including a sink with running water and a boiler of some sort, preferably electric, for heating water and for boiling barley, linseed and other feeds. A storage cupboard is required for items such as oil, salts, other additives, and cooking utensils.

The muck heap

Manure is a valuable bi-product of the stable's activities and is much sought after by mushroom growers and market gardeners. Whilst it is an excellent fertiliser under most conditions it must never be spread on horse pastures for fear of spreading the eggs of internal parasites.

The muck heap must be close at hand to avoid carrying soiled bedding over long distances. It should be sited downwind of the stables and dwellings. Easy access must be given to enable heavy vehicles to remove its contents from time to time.

The most convenient design for a muck heap is a concrete base with three retaining walls of concrete blocks forming a hollow square. The size of the muck heap depends entirely on the number of horses being kept and the frequency with which it is emptied.

Stable Bedding

Horses like to rest lying down and should be encouraged to do so. It is a sign of a relaxed, contented horse if he lies down in his stable for part of the day.

Stable bedding must fulfil a number of requirements: it must provide a warm comfortable bed and protect the horse from injury; it must not be injurious if eaten; it must be absorbent; it must be easily and regularly obtainable and economical to use; and it is an advantage if it can be disposed of easily and profitably after use.

Various materials can be used to make a stable bed, each with its own advantages and disadvantages.

Straw

This is the most widely used and easily obtainable type of bedding, and is most economical if it is purchased off the field at harvest time. It is then best to store it for six months before it is used. During this time it should be kept dry, aired and free from vermin.

Straw provides a warm, comfortable, easily maintained and handled bed. It is light in colour and drains well, has a pleasing appearance when laid as a bed, and has the added advantage that, when rotted down on the muck heap, it is readily purchased by market gardeners as fertiliser.

Straw is available in three types:

1 Wheat straw, which is the most popular as it provides a good bed which horses are unlikely to eat.
2 Oat straw, which makes a satisfactory bed though horses are inclined to eat it.
3 Barley straw which makes a less satisfactory bed as it has less spring and gets rather soggy. It also contains barley awns which may irritate the horse and cause him to rub.

As all straw is now combine harvested it tends to be short, which makes it rather more difficult to handle but does make it easier for the horse to move around in his box.

Wood shavings and sawdust

These both make a good bed, being light, soft, easy to handle and often inexpensive to those who live near a saw mill or timber works from which they can be collected. They are particularly favoured by the veterinary profession because they do not contain the spores found in straw that can cause respiratory problems in some horses. Horses that suffer from emphysematous conditions are best kept on wood shavings or sawdust.

The disadvantages of using wood shavings are that when soiled they are difficult to dispose of, they are unwanted as fertiliser and difficult to burn. They can be spread on the land, which requires specialist machinery, but never on horse pastures as this may well spread the eggs of internal parasites.

Peat moss

This makes a good bed but it is dark, heavy and expensive. It is however easy to dispose of to gardeners.

Sand

Sand is used as bedding in some countries but is is not entirely satisfactory. It compacts down hard and provides little or no warmth. Sand colic can ensue if horses eat it.It is usually cheap and easy to obtain but seashore sand should not be used as horses tend to lick it for its salty taste.

There are three other materials – shredded paper, bracken and bark strippings – that can be used to make stable beds, but they are not recommended except in extreme cases where more conventional forms of bedding cannot be obtained.

All stable beds should be thoroughly mucked out once a day. In this process, normally done first thing in the morning, all the droppings and wet bedding are removed and the dry bedding either piled in one corner of the box or put back down as a day bed. Fresh bedding is added as required, usually at the end of the afternoon when the bed is put down for the night. It helps to keep the stable fresh and to conserve bedding if the droppings are picked up regularly thoroughout the day.

As an alternative to this form of stable bedding, horses are often kept on deep litter. This consists of a permanent bed of about six inches of woodshavings, sawdust or peat moss with a thick straw bed on top of it. The droppings are picked up regularly and thoroughly but the bed is not mucked out daily. Fresh straw is added to the bed as required to keep it soft and comfortable. This system provides a warm, comfortable and economical bed. The entire bed is removed two or three times a year and replaced. Great care must be taken of horses' feet when they are kept on deep litter. Regular picking out and disinfecting of the foot, particularly in the area of the frog, will discourage thrush from forming.

Stable Routine

The routine of any stable will vary to suit individual requirements and to fit in with the programme demanded by the purpose for which the horses are kept. Nevertheless, there are set tasks which must be carried out every day to ensure the well-being of the horses, which is the purpose of all stable management. On a hunting, racing or competition day, or on the day after any of these activities, the routine will change but horses, being creatures of habit, do best when kept on a regular routine. The following is a suggested programme which covers the essential daily duties, but can be adjusted to suit individual situations.

7.00am   Fit the head collar and tie the horse up.
            Check him over to see that he is well and has not
            sustained any injuries during the night.
            Adjust the rugs.
            Clean and refill the water bucket.
            Muck out.
            Pick out the feet.
            Quarter (see page 114).
            Remove the head collar.
            Feed.

9.00am   Put on the head collar and tie the horse up.
            Remove the droppings.
            Remove rugs and saddle up.

9.00am   Exercise.
             On return from exercise, remove the saddle and
             bridle and put on the head collar, pick out the feet,
             water and allow the horse to roll.
             Rug up.
             Give first hay net.
             Remove the head collar.

11.30am   Put on the head collar and tie him up.
             Remove the droppings.
             Give a thorough grooming.
             Put on day rugs.
             Check the water bucket.
             Remove the head collar.
             Give second feed.
             Tidy the stable yard.

2.00pm   Remove the droppings.
             Fill the water bucket.
             Give second hay net.
             Clean tack, head collar etc.

5.00pm   Put on his head collar and tie him up.
             Remove the droppings.
             Pick out the feet.
             Shake up the bedding and add fresh straw as
             required.
             Change from day rugs to night rugs.
             Fill the water bucket.
             Give third feed.
             Remove the head collar.

9.00pm   Remove the droppings.
             Fill the water bucket.
             Shake up the bedding.
             Check the rugs.
             Put in the final, and largest, hay net.

Stable Vices

Occasionally, horses that have been badly trained or subjected to
poor stable management develop some form of stable vice. Once
these vices are established they are very difficult to cure.

Crib biting and gnawing the woodwork
This is particularly irritating as it not only spoils the stable but it may well lead to the more serious vice of 'wind sucking' (see below). It is very tempting for the horse to chew on fresh, unseasoned pine wood which is often used in modern stable construction. Any wooden edge that invites the horse to chew should be covered with metal. Other timber should be treated thoroughly with a strong creosote solution. Mangers that offer a horse an edge to chew should be avoided.

A permanent, small hay net may occupy the horse sufficiently to distract him from chewing the woodwork but boredom is often the cause of this vice and the most effective way to discourage it is to keep the horse busy and to ensure that he is worked really well every day.

Eating the bedding and droppings
Both these practices may be due to a lack of bulk, fibre and salt in the diet. If necessary, the bedding should be changed from straw to wood shavings or peat – horses seldom eat either of these. If the horse must be kept on straw the bed can be sprinkled liberally with a strong disinfectant solution. It may also help to keep the new and and the old bedding well mixed up.

To discourage the eating of droppings they should be picked out of the box regularly. A salt lick hung permanently in the stable may help to dissuade the horse from this undesirable habit.

Wind sucking
The horse seizes the manger or woodwork between his incisor teeth, leans back and sucks in air. It is not only very detrimental to the horse, causing deterioration and loss of condition, but is difficult to cure, and horses that suffer from this unsoundness should be avoided. Most treatment proves useless but there are a number of approaches that are worth trying:

1 Ensure that the horse is not bored and that he is getting sufficient exercise.
2 Any protrusion in the stable on which he can take a hold should be removed. Some horses in the advanced stages of this problem can wind suck without holding on to anything.
3 A thick leather strap fitted fairly tightly round the neck, just

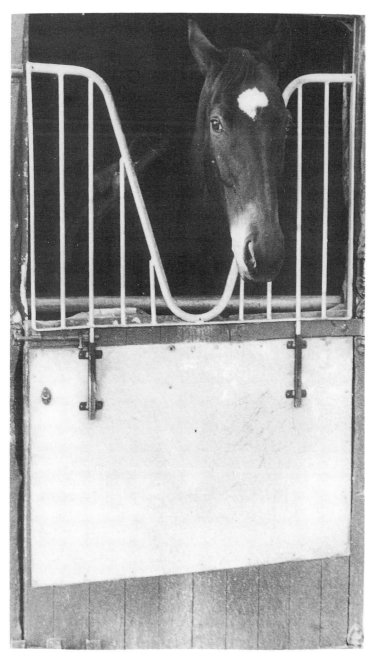

Plate 14 The anti-weaving grille

behind the ears, sometimes discourages a horse from wind sucking. A good saddler can supply a 'cribbing strap' which has a metal insert that fits into the gullet. This is more effective than a plain leather strap.

4 A simple veterinary operation now exists to relieve this condition which appears to be successful in many cases.

Weaving

The horse stands with his head over the stable door and rocks from side to side, sometimes so violently that one foot is lifted off the ground with each rocking movement. The cause is usually boredom and insufficient work. If the horse is worked hard enough daily, he should not want to weave on return to his box. Once the habit is formed, however, it is hard to break. The top door of the box should be kept shut or a grille fitted so that the horse can look out but not lean over the door. Alternatively, an anti-weaving frame can be fitted to the top of the door which allows the horse to put his head out but not to weave from side to side.

When possible the horse should be turned out to grass. It is very seldom that a horse is seen weaving in a field. This practice is often copied by other horses in a yard so it is important that an offending horse is either stopped or isolated.

Kicking and biting

Horses that either kick or bite usually do so because they are frightened or have been badly handled. A timid or frightened groom may cause a horse to be nervous. Whilst care should always be taken when moving round a horse in his box, confident, bold handling usually cures a horse that has a reputation as a kicker or a biter. When the horse kicks or bites he must be reprimanded immediately with a quick slap and growl combined. It is no use going away to get a whip and coming back to slap the horse two minutes later. He must be allowed to attempt to kick or bite again and given a quick slap as he does so. He must associate this slap with his offence. The 'association of ideas' is an important principle in all the horse's training.

Keeping the Horse at Grass

Horses are wasteful, inefficient and consequently uneconomical grazers. They therefore require a good deal of supervision when they are kept at grass. It is a mistake to think of a paddock as just a field where the horse can be kept safely without requiring too much attention. Whilst at grass he is permanently at risk from disease, injury, the weather, vandals, thieves and himself. The field in which the horse is kept should be treated not only as a safe place but as a valuable source of food and the grass should be treated like any other crop.

If the field has well-drained, fertile soil producing a variety of grass and some clover, one acre will support one horse if the management of the grass is good. Horse paddocks are, unfortunately, seldom of high-quality grazing and it is more likely that one and a half acres will be required per horse.

A good horse paddock requires:

1 A good mixture of grasses and herbs (see Plates 15–18). Basic pasture grasses include: perennial ryegrass; cocksfoot; timothy. Palatable turf-forming grasses include: creeping red fescue; crested dog's tail; rough-stalked meadow grass on wet land; smooth-stalked meadow grass on dry land; browntop, for making turf only. Another very palatable grass is tall fescue, which is nutritious but forms no turf.

  Desirable herbs include: wild white clover; chicory; burnet; ribgrass; sheep's parsley; yarrow; dandelion. Herbs can be introduced into a paddock by direct drilling, or the seed can be broadcast, harrowed and rolled. They are best sown in July/August, and the paddock then left until the following spring, or in April with the paddock left until August.

2 Sound fencing. Post and rail is best but expensive. Hedges can be satisfactory but are often insecure and require a lot of maintenance. Post and wire is just acceptable but is potentially dangerous; barbed wire is dangerous and unacceptable. Field gates must be secure and easy to use, particularly when one is carrying buckets, or riding or leading a horse.

3 A water supply. The horse requires 36–45 litres (8–10 gal) of water a day. A running stream is ideal, provided that it has a stone or gravel bottom and is clear, unpolluted water. Brackish or stagnant pond water is of no value as horses will not drink it.

Plate 15 Rough-stalked meadow grass

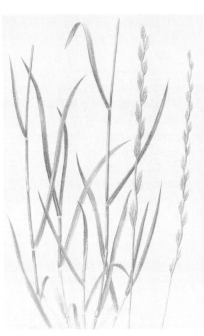

Plate 16 Perennial ryegrass

Plate 17 Cocksfoot

Plate 18 Timothy grass

Plate 19 An excellent post-and-rail fence

Plate 20 These iron park railings have stood for nearly one hundred years

Plate 21 A dangerous fence

Plate 22 A water trough built to last

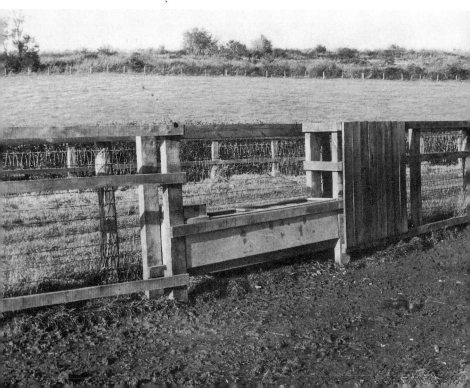

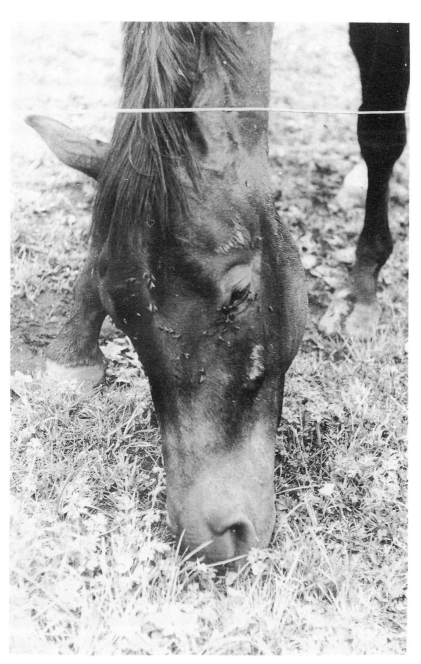

Plate 23 The height of discomfort

The best system of supplying water is through a galvanised iron trough with a covered ball cock. It should be set into a concrete hard standing to prevent a bog from forming around it. It is also sensible to lag those parts of the supply pipes that are exposed, to prevent freezing in winter.

4 Shelter. A shelter is needed to provide protection from flies and the sun in the summer and cold wind, rain and snow in the winter. A copse of trees or a thick, high hedge will provide some shelter but they are no substitute for a three-sided field shelter.

5 Drainage. A wet field requires drainage if it is to be at its most productive. Grass does not grow well in very wet conditions and horses cause a lot of damage on very wet ground.

6 Fertilising. Grass, like any other crop, needs to be fed. In early March and again in mid-summer 1 to 2 bags of Fisons Regular (20:10:10) should be applied per acre. This will supply in the correct ratio the essential foods that the grass requires: nitrogen, phosphate and potash. It will ensure continuous grass production throughout the growing season from May until about October. The local officer of the Ministry of Agriculture, Fisheries and Food will provide a soil analysis if provided with ten soil samples taken at a depth of about four inches, from various parts of the field. As a result of this analysis he will be able to advise on the type of fertiliser that should be used and the quantity required.

Three or four weeks should pass before horses are put out onto a newly fertilised field, allowing sufficient time for the rain to wash the fertiliser well into the ground.

7 Worm control. All horse paddocks suffer from worm infestation, which should be kept to a minimum by:

(a) Worming the horses regularly with a proprietary brand of 'wormer'. The veterinary surgeon will give advice on the type that should be used.

(b) Picking up the droppings daily or at least twice a week.

(c) Sharing the grazing with a few sheep or bullocks. The horse worm larvae are killed in the digestive tract of sheep or bullocks without causing them any harm.

(d) Harrowing, which exposes the worm larvae to sunlight and is a very effective way of destroying them.

(e) Keeping horses in for forty-eight hours after they have been wormed. This ensures that worm-infested droppings are not expelled into the field.

8 Weed control. Heavy infestation of weeds discourages the growth of grass. Some, such as ragwort, are poisonous to horses. Docks and nettles are difficult to remove once they are established; they are unsightly in a horse paddock and are a sign of bad husbandry. To allow weeds to spread to other properties may constitute an offence under the Control of Weeds Act. Some weeds can be destroyed by spraying, but any poison in a horse paddock is a potential danger. The most effective way to dispose of ragwort, docks and nettles is to pull them up and burn them; the best way to discourage other weeds is to encourage the growth of the grass.

9 Mowing, harrowing and rolling. Horses are very selective grazers and will not feed around piles of droppings, where other horses regularly stale or where the grass has grown long and gone to seed. To ensure that maximum use is made of the field it is necessary to 'top' it regularly, ie mow it lightly to remove the long or rank grass. Grass clippings should never be fed to horses as they foment in the gut and cause very serious colic.

Harrowing is required to pull out dead vegetation and to aerate the soil. This should be done at the end of February each year.

Rolling compresses the surface of the soil and packs the soil down around the roots of the grass to assist in healthy growth.

Whenever possible grazing should be 'rotated', ie divided into two or more areas with one part being rested for eight weeks or so, while the horses use another. This enables the grass to grow and ensures efficient grazing in a small area.

The term 'horse sick' is an expression used to describe a neglected paddock where the grass is over-grazed and there are patches of docks, nettles and ragwort. The fencing is usually poor with makeshift water troughs and gates, and the addition of a few littered show jumps creates a scene of sordid neglect. Horse paddocks require a good deal of attention if they are to remain productive and a credit to their owners.

Plate 24 The 'horse-sick' pasture

Plate 25 A poor, dangerous fence

Plate 26 A dangerous field mate

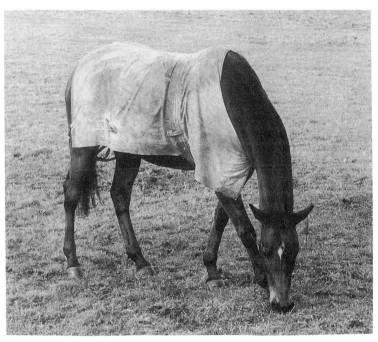

Plate 27 A well-used New Zealand rug

The horse kept at grass requires:

1 Regular inspection. At least once a day he should be visited to ensure that he is well and has not sustained any injury. If he is wearing a New Zealand rug this may need to be adjusted.
2 Worming (see pages 92–4).
3 Feeding. From October until about May, when the grass is not growing and there is little nutrition in what is left of the summer grass, the horse requires supplementary feeding. The type of food and the quantity depend on the type of work that he is required to do.
4 Attention to his feet. The feet require regular picking out and trimming. If he is shod then the normal care of the shod foot will be necessary (see pages 99–104).
5 Grooming. If he is regularly ridden for enjoyment or for competition he needs to be groomed and to have mane and tail tidied. This will not be the thorough grooming that would be given to the stabled horse but sufficient to keep him looking clean, tidy and cared for. It should be remembered that the natural oil found in the horse's coat provides him with protection against cold and wet weather and should not be removed entirely. There are some styles of clip that are suitable for the grass-kept horse, enabling him to be worked but leaving sufficient coat on to give some protection for most of the year (see pages 114–18).

Turning the horse out to grass
Most horses benefit from a rest period out at grass at least once a year. This depends upon the type of work in which they are employed and the intensity of that work.

A horse that has been hunted for three days a fortnight from November to March will almost certainly be turned out to grass from April until September, when he is brought in to be prepared for the next season. Show jumpers, polo ponies, horse trial horses and show horses are nearly all rested at grass between seasons. There are a few horses who do not do well when they are turned out for a rest, but these are the exception rather than the rule. These may benefit from living in, and being turned out for part of the day.

The period for which the horse is rested must be decided upon by the owner to fit in with his riding or competition arrangements. Some horses are turned out during the day and brought into the stable at night. Others are let down completely and allowed to revert to their natural state with some supplementary feeding, depending on the weather and the quality of the available grass.

Any change in the horse's environment must be made gradually, to avoid abrupt changes to the diet, work, grooming and surrounding conditions. When the horse is to be turned out to grass at the end of a busy season, a programme on the following lines is appropriate, though it should be adjusted to suit the individual horse in a particular situation:

First week   Replace half the concentrates in the diet with hay.
Hack out daily for one hour.
Turn him out in the field in a New Zealand rug for two hours per day.
Leave the top door of the stable open at night.
Reduce grooming to quartering only.
Worm him.
Check the field regarding security, fencing and gates; poisonous plants; dangerous litter; holes; hay rack and feed manger; water supply.

Second week   Replace half the remaining concentrates in the diet with hay.
Hack out daily for three quarters of an hour.
Turn him out in a New Zealand rug for two or three hours per day.
Leave the top door of the stable open at night and remove one rug.
No grooming, quartering only.
Rasp teeth if necessary.
Check that tetanus antitoxin injection and influenza immunisation are up to date.

Third week   Cease exercise, turn him out to grass during the day and bring him in at night.
Give a small feed and a hay net each evening.

Third week   Cease grooming except for picking out the feet morning and evening.

Remove the shoes.

Take off all the rugs at night except in severe weather.

At the end of this week turn him out into the field permanently, unless delayed by really bad weather.

Bringing the horse up from grass

When the horse is brought in from grass after a period of rest, a similar programme should be followed for the reverse process:

First week   Give a small daily feed in the field, perhaps 0.9kg (2lb) of oats.

Prepare the stable.

Ensure that there are stocks of bedding, hay and short feed.

Check rugs, tack, clipping machine and first-aid cabinet.

Make an appointment to have him shod at the start of the third week.

Second week   Continue to give the small daily feed in the field.

Bring him in at night and turn him out during the day.

Give a hay net at night.

Third week   Bring him in full time.

Clip, and start grooming.

Have him shod.

Start slow work, walking only for half an hour a day at first.

Check that tack, especially the girth and saddle, is supple and not likely to rub the soft, fat horse.

Start to build up the concentrates in the diet very slowly, reducing the bulk gradually as the concentrates increase.

Worm him.

Rasp teeth if necessary.

Check that tetanus antitoxin injection and influenza immunisation are up to date.

Getting the Horse Fit

Like the human athlete the horse will perform his task better and last longer if he is prepared for competition with a well thought out, progressive plan (see overleaf).

To ask a horse to gallop, jump and compete without the necessary preparation is to court disaster. The horse, in his natural environment and without a rider, is quite capable of galloping and jumping but in order to get the best possible performance from, say, a hunter, show jumper, eventer or polo pony he must be carefully trained and prepared. Each horse is an individual and the training programme must be designed to suit the requirements of a particular animal and the discipline for which he is being prepared. There are, however, various considerations common to all fitness programmes:

General administration
Shoeing.
Clipping.
Veterinary care – worming, anti-tetanus injections, teeth rasping etc.
Grooming and strapping.

Feeding
Concentrates.
Bulk.
Green food.
Additives.

Work and exercise
Conditioning.
Schooling.
Jumping.
Wind.
Competition.
Retention of condition during the hunting or competition season.

Fitness programme

The following programme is a suggested outline for getting a serious hunter or competition horse fit over a period of twelve to fifteen weeks. It assumes that the horse starts completely unfit, having just come up from grass. Some horses take longer to reach peak fitness than others. Young horses generally take longer than more mature horses that have been trained to competition fitness before. The programme is a very broad, rule-of-thumb guide which should be adjusted to achieve the best results from each particular horse.

	Conditioning period (4–5 wks)	Hardening up period (4–5 wks)	Period for improving the horse's wind (4–5 wks)	Retention of fitness during season (12 wks)
Work & exercise	Walk and slow trot ¾–2 hr daily.	Road work 2 hr. Slow canters. School work ie suppling and gymnastic exercises. Light cub hunting.	Long canters 12 mins. Gallops 1¼ miles slow; ¾ mile fast; ½ mile slow down. Jump schooling.	Keep fresh. Reduce road work. Lead out in hand. Pipe openers. Hacking out.
Feeding	Oats 1·8–3·6kg (4–8lb). Bran 1·3–1·8kg (3–4lb). Hay 4·5–5·4kg (10–12lb). Daily, plus green food, horse cubes or mixes.	Oats 4·5–7·2kg (10–16lb). Bran 0·9–1·3kg (2–3lb). Hay 6·3kg (14lb). Daily, plus vitamins, horse cubes or mixes and linseed.	Decrease hay to 4·5kg (10lb). Maintain concentrate element of diet.	Keep diet appetising by giving some variety and including succulents such as molasses, green food, apples or root vegetables.
Administration	Shoeing, clipping, teeth rasping, influenza and anti-tetanus inoculations. Grooming and strapping.	Continue grooming and strapping. Attend to shoeing.	Continue grooming and strapping. Attend to shoeing.	Continue grooming and strapping. Watch for signs of staleness or boredom eg loss of appetite, loss of condition or enthusiasm, dull coat, listlessness.

Day of first competition or opening meet

3 Feeding the Horse

Careful, thoughtful feeding is a most important part of stable management, particularly for the competition horse who is subjected to a good deal of unnatural strain.

In order to feed the horse efficiently and economically it is necessary to know something about his natural feeding habits and requirements. In his natural state he would spend his life grazing on grassy plains, feeding for most of the day. Because the horse's digestive system is designed to take in and process great quantities of cellulose on a fairly constant basis he has developed a small stomach for his overall size which can cope with the constant provision of small amounts but not with large feeds and long intervals in between them. This gives rise to the necessity to offer horses small feeds at frequent intervals. Three feeds a day are acceptable but four or five are better. Horses are creatures of habit and do best if they are fed regularly and at the same times each day. Only the very best forage should be used. It is false economy to buy inferior food as this can cause colic, which is distressing, painful and sometimes fatal.

In order to obtain the maximum value from his food the horse should be watered before he is fed, otherwise his digestion may be impaired and some of the food value wasted. A period of at least one hour, better two, should be allowed to elapse after he has been fed before he is worked or exercised. This allows him to digest his food properly and reduces the risk of colic. Horses, like humans, appreciate some variety in their diet and should be fed something succulent every day.

The amount and type of food that the horse requires depends on his size, type, stage of training and the work that he is required to do. If, for any reason, a change is made in the diet it should be made gradually, as abrupt changes can be harmful.

As a very broad guide, a horse requires 2.5 per cent of his body weight in food per day. Therefore a horse weighing 455kg (1,000lb) will require about 11kg (25lb) of food daily. As a general rule, half of this should be roughage (hay, bran, etc) and half concentrates, (oats, barley, etc). The horse in hard work will require more concentrates and less bulk. The horse in light work will do best on fewer concentrates and rather more bulk.

To assess the weight of a horse, if it is not possible to weigh him, this formula will give a reasonably accurate guide:

$$\frac{\text{Girth}^2 \times \text{length}}{300} = \text{Total weight in pounds}$$

The girth measurement is taken round the barrel in inches. The length is from the elbow to the point of the buttock in inches. These are very broad rules and must be intelligently applied to each horse to ensure that he is fed the right type of food in the correct amount.

To ensure efficient and economical management, the reasons for feeding the horse should be clearly understood. Food is required to: provide energy; provide for growth in young animals; replace body tissue broken down by daily wear and tear; maintain the body temperature. If each of these requirements is fulfilled the result should be a well fed, economically maintained horse.

Clearly, some horses require more energy-giving foods than others. Young horses need protein to ensure healthy growth; horses working long hours every day require rations of maintain them in that work; those working once or twice a week require less.

Up to 30 per cent of the horse's food goes to maintain body temperature. In cold weather those out at grass may need an increase in rations. Stabled horses may need less food if their rugs are well fitted, the beds are well laid and draughts are excluded.

Horses in work are usually given one rest day a week, maybe after hunting or some other strenuous event. They will almost certainly be led out in hand for twenty to thirty minutes to stretch their legs and, where conditions permit, possibly turned out to grass for an hour or so in a New Zealand rug, depending on the weather. Feeds on rest days, or any other period of enforced rest, must be adjusted to suit the circumstances. The rest day is a good time to feed a bran mash, but in any case it is essential to cut down on the concentrate part of the diet when the horse is off work, and to increase the roughage element. Failure to do this may cause a very serious condition called azoturia on return to work. This condition, sometimes known as 'set-fast' or 'tying up', is muscle and blood vessel paralysis caused by exercising a horse after a period of rest during which a full concentrate ration has been fed.

Practical Feeding
The traditional diet of the stabled horse consists of oats, bran and hay. These ingredients provide all the nutritional requirements of the average working horse, if fed in the correct amounts and the appropriate ratio. Modern research into animal nutrition has enabled horse food manufacturers to make feeding more efficient, economical and easy. The horse's daily ration may include some, but probably not all, of the following types of food.

Oats
Oats are the best energy-giving food for horses, and are easily digested and palatable. They should be free from dust or dirt, plump, heavy and without noticeable smell. To extract the most value from oats they should be either bruised, rolled, crushed or crimped. This breaks the hard shell of the seed, allowing the digestive juices to get at the kernel. If this is not done there is a possibility that the seed will be passed intact through the digestive system and wasted. Oats are a heating food and should be fed with care to high spirited horses and ponies. Too many oats may make such animals difficult rides.

Bran
Bran is what is left when the flour is milled from wheat. It is high in protein and is excellent for adding to the oat ration to provide bulk. Modern milling techniques reduce bran almost to a powder. It is best, however, if it is in a broad, dry flake with some flour. Being very high in phosphorus, bran may cause a problem if it is fed in quantity to young stock: if the phosphorus/calcium ratio is out of balance in the diet of young, growing animals the formation and growth of bone may be impaired.

A bran mash is very useful as a laxative on a horse's rest day, or when he is on a low concentrate diet as a result of injury or sickness, and is a vital element in sick nursing (see pages 74, 94). To make a bran mash, fill one third of a plastic bucket with bran and add boiling water until the bran is 'crumble' dry but not wet and sloppy or too dry to eat. Stir well and add 15g (½oz) of salt. A handful of oats, a chopped apple or a little treacle will make the mash more appetising; 600ml (1 pint) of cooked linseed may be added or 115g (4oz) of Epsom salts as a laxative. Once the mash has been made, it should be covered with a cloth and left to cool to an edible temperature before it is fed.

Hay
Hay is dried grass. If it is made well it enables valuable animal food stocks to be kept during the winter months. It falls broadly into two types: meadow hay, which is cut from a natural pasture on which the grass has been allowed to go to seed; and seed hay, which is grown from a specially planted mixture of grasses with some clover.

Meadow hay is cheaper than seed hay, softer and less nutritious. It is excellent for ponies and horses that are not subjected to the rigours of hunting or competition riding. Seed hay is more expensive, harder and more nutritious, being rich in protein and fibre. It is more suitable for racehorses, competition horses and hunters. Whichever variety is used it should be: clean and free from dust or mould; brownish green in colour; sweet smelling; a good mixture of grasses, free from weeds or thistles; made when the seed has formed but before the seed has dropped; about 44 bales to the ton.

Hay that is very tangled in the bale indicates that it has been turned several times. This may mean that it was made in wet weather and that most of the seed has been shaken out. It is best if the individual stalks are lying straight and regular.

Hay should not be fed to horses until it is at least six months old. Seed hay is much better if it is stored until it is a year old and meadow hay until it is eighteen months old. It can be fed in a variety of ways:

1 On the stable floor. This is the most natural way for the horse to feed but there is the possibility that it will be trodden into the bedding and wasted.
2 In a hay rack. This is a good, economical, time-saving method. If the rack is too high the seeds may drop into the horse's eyes.
3 In a hay net. This is an accurate and economical way of feeding hay, as it can easily be weighed and washed. Filling hay nets is

time consuming and an empty hay net left hanging in a stable can be dangerous; it must be hung sufficiently high to ensure that the horse cannot catch his foot in it when the hay has been eaten.

Horses that suffer from problems in their wind benefit from having their hay soaked in water for twelve hours before it is fed. This washes out the dust and spores found in hay which are the main causes of emphysematous conditions in the horse. Most horses prefer their hay to be dampened a little before it is fed.

To provide bulk in the feed 'chaff' or 'chop' is sometimes added. This is hay, or sometimes oat straw, that has been chopped into pieces an inch or two in length. It is good for horses that bolt their food as it tends to slow them down. Only good quality hay should be made into chaff; it is a mistake to dispose of poor quality hay in this way.

Hay can be fed in measured amounts at set times in the day or, if finances permit, a full hay net can be left in the stable all the time, so that the horse has hay available as and when he needs it. If hay is fed at regular times, it is usually given in two or three lots a day. This will depend on individual stables and routines. The usual practice is to feed a small hay net in the morning after work, whilst the horse is being groomed; another after lunch when most well-run stables are quiet and resting; and the last, and largest, at about 9pm to last through the night.

Good hay is not only very nutritious, but has a very good therapeutic value, as pulling at a hay net keeps horses content and helps to relieve boredom. Horses fed on a diet that excludes hay often develop stable vices which are difficult to cure. These include crib biting, bedding eating, wind sucking and eating the droppings or stable clothing, all of which are very undesirable.

As an alternative to hay a number of vacuum-packed, wilted grass feeds are available. They are sold under various brand names and are designed to replace hay in the horses's diet. These products have also been fed successfully to other livestock. Only best quality long grass is used, cut when at its best and in full seed but before the seed has fallen. The grass is allowed to wilt, not killed as it would be when made into hay, and baled. The bales are then chemically treated to prevent heating taking place, compressed to half their size and packed into strong plastic bags.

In this controlled environment the irritant spores normally found in hay are unable to form. The result is a succulent, nutritious, sweet-smelling food which horses eat enthusiastically, sometimes after a short introductory period. It is a little more expensive than hay and once a plastic bag has been opened its contents must be used within a few days; the shelf life of an opened bag is short.

Horse cubes and mixes

A variety of compounded horse feeds is available. These feeds are produced as cubes or mixes. The cubes range from 'horse and pony cubes' through 'stud cubes' right up to the highly nutritious 'racehorse cubes'. Horse cubes are easy to feed and ensure a balanced diet of high quality food. Each type of cube is the product of careful research into the nutritional requirements of the horse in particular circumstances. The well compounded cube consists of a balance of protein, fat, carbohydrate, vitamins and trace elements.

Whilst it is extravagant to add horse cubes to conventional feed, there is a possibility that a diet of horse cubes alone will become monotonous. To give some variety it helps to add something succulent to each feed – root vegetables, apples or fresh green food will make the diet more appetising without upsetting the nutritional balance.

The mixes contain cereals, oats, barley, maize, etc with an appetising additive such as molasses.

Both horse cubes and mixes, though a very convenient means of feeding, will prove more expensive than conventional feed. Like all items of forage they should be stored in vermin-proof containers. The shelf life is limited, particularly where bags of cubes are piled on top of one another. It is sensible therefore not to buy a greater quantity than is required at any one time. Recommended feed scales for horses of various sizes are printed on each pack, based upon the type of work on which the horses are employed.

Dried sugar beet

This is obtainable in pulp form or in cubes. It is almost entirely cellulose and sugar and is good for putting flesh on thin horses or keeping flesh on horses in slow work. It is not suitable for horses in hard, fast work. Sugar beet pulp or cubes must never be fed dry as this may cause the horse to choke and once in the stomach will absorb all the available liquid and swell up considerably. Sugar beet must be soaked thoroughly before it is fed until it has absorbed at least twice its own volume of water, which takes about twelve hours. A reasonable amount is 450g (1lb) in each feed, up to a total of 1.3kg (3lb) in any one day. Once it has been soaked it must be used, as it will ferment and deteriorate rapidly.

Flaked maize
This is high in energy value but is fattening and heating. It should only be fed in small amounts, less than 20 per cent of the total concentrate ration of horses in hard work.

Linseed
This is the seed of the flax plant. It is very nutritious, being rich in protein and oil.

To improve condition and to give gloss to the coat linseed can be fed as either 'jelly' or 'tea'. The seed is never fed unsoaked or unboiled as it is thought to be poisonous to horses in the raw state. It is sufficient to feed it twice a week. About 225g (8oz) of uncooked seed is sufficient for a horse of about 15.2 hands high.

The measured amount of seed should be soaked in water for twelve hours. After this time, more water is added and brought to the boil. It should then be allowed to cool and the resultant jelly added to the feed. To make linseed tea, the same procedure is followed but more water is used. The water in which the linseed is boiled is highly nutritious and can be fed with bran as a linseed mash.

Barley
Crushed, rolled or flaked barley can be fed as a substitute for oats. The food value is similar to that of oats but it does not have the same energy giving or heating effect.

Boiled barley is fed warm with bran. It is fattening and useful for tempting shy feeders to eat. It is particularly useful after a hard day's hunting or competing and as part of the diet of a stale or over-worked horse it can be fed to give variety and to provide energy without over-heating. It should be brought to the boil and simmered for four to six hours until the grains split. Barley burns easily, so it must be carefully watched during its preparation.

Beans

Dried beans when split are nutritious but very heating. They provide variety in the stabled horse's diet and are usefully fed to horses and ponies that are wintering out. Two handfuls twice a day, mixed with other feed, would be an acceptable ration.

The way in which the horse eats is often an indication as to his well-being. The healthy horse will look forward to his food and will be ready and waiting for it at set times each day. He will eat it with relish, but without bolting it.

Sometimes the horse will drop food from his mouth whilst masticating it. This is known as 'quidding' and may be due to malformation of the teeth or some injury to the mouth. In these circumstances veterinary advice should be sought.

As the horse masticates his food the teeth of the upper and lower jaws grind together in a circular motion, causing the edges of the molar teeth to become very sharp. About twice yearly it is necessary to rasp away the sharp edges as they may discourage the horse from masticating his food sufficiently. This is a simple task that can be done by the veterinary surgeon or the experienced layman.

When the horse who normally eats up well suddenly goes off his food there is a reason that must be identified and rectified. It may be that he is sickening for some illness, a cold or a similar infection, or he may be suffering from colic. The food may be musty. A change in circumstances in the yard can also be the cause: perhaps he has been moved to another loose box, or the horse next to him is bullying him at feed times.

Uneaten food should not be left in the manger for too long. If the horse is clearly not going to eat it, it must be removed and the manger cleaned out ready for the next feed. It may not be serious if the horse leaves one feed only but, as with any change in his normal behaviour, to be 'off his feed' is almost certainly a sign that something is wrong.

'Shy feeders' are not uncommon. They are horses that are reluctant to eat. There are many factors that may cause this situation, including bad grooms and poor preparation of the food. A skilled groom will be able to tempt the shy feeder to eat by varying the diet, offering frequent small feeds, ensuring that the horse is not disturbed whilst eating, etc. Careful, considerate

The horse's ration and breakdown of feeds

This is a typical feeding scale for a 15·3 hands high, seven-year-old horse that is hacked out for one to two hours daily, six days a week. He is hunted twice a fortnight in winter and competes from time to time, at a modest level, in summer. The horse is stabled, a good doer and of steady temperament. Such a feed scale can be only a guide. It must be applied carefully and thoughtfully to suit the individual horse's condition, physique, workload and temperament.

Amounts are based on the assumption that the horse of 15·3 hands high weighs approximately 500kg (1,100lb) and therefore requires about 2·5 per cent of his body weight in food per day, ie 12·5kg (27½lb). Of this, half should be concentrates (energy giving foods) and half roughage (foods that provide bulk). Some elements in the diet provide both concentrates and roughage. In this case as the horse is not in particularly hard work the concentrates have been reduced and the roughage increased.

Time	Oats	Boiled barley	Flaked maize	Bran	Chaff	Carrot/ green food	Hay	Other	Remarks
6.30am	0·9kg (2lb)			450g (1lb)	225g (½lb)				Small feed before work
10.00am							1·1kg (2½lb)		
12.30pm	0·9kg (2lb)	450g (1lb)		450g (1lb)	225g (½lb)	225g (½lb)		25g (1oz) cod liver or vegetable oil	
2.00pm							1·1kg (2½lb)		
5.30pm	0·9kg (2lb)	450g (1lb)		450g (1lb)	225g (½lb)	225g (½lb)			
9.00pm	1·3kg (3lb)	225g (½lb)	225g (½lb)	450g (1lb)	225g (½lb)	225g (½lb)	1·3kg (3lb)		Largest feed at the end of the day
Totals	Concentrates 5·4kg (12lb)						Roughage 7kg (15½lb)		

feeding and use of the imagination are often the best ways to solve this problem.

Watering the Horse

The constant provision of cold, fresh water is a vital element of good stable management and horsemastership. The various means of providing water for the stabled horse are covered in Chapter 2. The following principles should be observed:

1 The water provided must be clean, fresh and cold.
2 Hard water is more acceptable than soft water.
3 Water should be given before feeding.
4 Water should not be given directly before exercise.
5 After strenuous exercise a small drink should be given at first and a longer drink later. After hunting, on a cold night, chilled water can be given but the temperature should not be over 26.5°C (80°F).
6 During continuous work a short drink should be given every two hours. The practice of letting the horse drink from a stream, with the bit in his mouth whilst the rider sits in the saddle with the girths done up is unacceptable. To water the horse, the rider must dismount, loosen the girth and take the bit out of the horse's mouth.
7 Horses being transported over long distances by road, air or sea, will require water every two hours.

4 Keeping the Horse Healthy

Signs of Health

To be able to recognise when a horse is ill or off colour the owner must be familiar with the signs of good health. A knowledge of what is normal will help to identify that which is abnormal.

The horse's general attitude should be bright and alert without being nervous. He will normally welcome a visitor to his box or at least recognise the visitor's presence.

He should stand with equal weight on each of his four legs, but will often rest a hind leg. When a foreleg is rested it usually means that it hurts, and needs to have the weight taken off it. However, this is not always the case – some horses rest a sound foreleg, which emphasises the need to know the normal ways of an individual in order that the abnormal can be quickly recognised.

The attitude of the horse's head and the look on his face are good indications of his overall well-being. The eye should be bright, clear and alert without weeping or discharge. The mucus membrane (the pink surround under the eyelids) should be a salmon-pink colour, not red and inflamed or white and anaemic looking. The ears should be mobile and attentive; ears that are permanently laid back are a sign of some disorder or distress. When the horse pricks his ears he is focusing both eyes on a single object, usually the sign of a bright alert horse. The nostrils should be open and without discharge, the mucus membrane again being salmon-pink in colour. The lips should be closed and the inside of the lips and gums should be of a similar colour to the membranes of the eyes and nostrils. The carriage of the head is an indication as to his state of health. The head hung low or raised in an unnatural way is often an indication that all is not well.

The body should be warm to the touch. A good way of checking whether or not the horse is cold is to feel his ears – if they are cold to the touch the horse is usually cold.

The coat should be soft and shining, and the skin soft and supple, moving freely over the underlying tissues. The skin should also be free from spots, lumps or sores. Bald patches or an unhealthy appearance of the mane and tail are indications that the horse is, in some way, unhealthy.

The legs should be without abnormal lumps and bumps. They should be cool to the touch, the back tendons being cold and hard. There should be no soreness or weeping at the back of the pastern or the heels. Hooves should be hard and cold, the sole of the foot dry and hard, and the frog well formed and springy. There must be no trace of a foul smell. At walk, trot and canter the horse should move freely and should show no signs of favouring one or more legs.

The healthy horse will pass droppings and stale without pain, effort or distress. On average the horse passes droppings about eight to ten times a day, and stales about five to six times a day. The consistency of the droppings should be that they are passed easily and break on hitting the ground. Urine should be almost colourless, odourless and passed without strain. Dark or rust-coloured urine is a sign of ill health as a rule.

The horse should eat with enthusiasm and drink from 36 to 45 litres (8 to 10gal) of water a day. However some horses are slow eaters, and they may leave some food and return to it later.

Temperature

The horse's temperature is taken in the rectum. To do this, grease the bulb end of the thermometer with a little vaseline and, lifting the horse's tail with one hand, insert the thermometer with a rotary action into the rectum. Do not let go of the thermometer and keep it inserted for about two minutes. After this time withdraw it and read the temperature from the graduated scale. The thermometer should then be washed and returned to its case.

As the horse's normal temperature is between 37.2°and 38.3°C (99° and 101°F) a rise of a degree should be considered abnormal and a rise of two or three degrees should be considered serious and requiring veterinary attention.

Pulse rate

The normal pulse rate at rest is 36 to 40 beats per minute. The easiest place to feel the pulse in the horse is just under the jaw

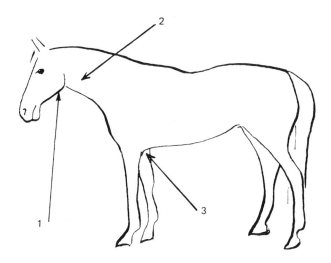

Fig 11 Areas in which the horse's pulse can be most easily felt: 1 the facial artery, under the jaw; 2 the carotid artery, on the neck near the jugular vein; 3 the median artery, behind the elbow

where the facial artery can be felt against the jaw bone. The pulse can also be felt at the carotid artery near the jugular vein in the neck or at the median artery behind the elbow.

Rate of respiration
The normal rate of respiration for the horse at rest is between 8 and 16 breaths per minute. The rate of breathing can best be seen by looking at the rib-cage from the rear. As the horse exhales the rib-cage should make one complete movement. If there is a double beat of the rib-cage as he exhales, this may be a sign that the horse has 'broken wind' which is an irreversible condition. This may not be obvious when the horse is at rest, so this examination should be made after the horse has been given a short gallop.

Veterinary Care
The stabled horse is kept in an unnatural environment, fed a comparatively unnatural diet and has considerable unnatural physical strain put upon him when he is ridden. Consequently he is subjected to numerous health risks. He is prone to digestive disorders, various infections, respiratory disorders and the effects of concussion on his limbs.

The horse owner must be able to tell when a horse is off colour, unwell or very ill, and must know how to treat minor ailments, when to call the veterinary surgeon (and what information to give on the telephone), and how to 'sick nurse' the horse.

The veterinary surgeon will want to know: the broad nature of the trouble; details of any injury; temperature, pulse and respiration rate; when dung and urine were last passed; when the horse last ate or drank. He should be called in when:

1 The horse is clearly in distress, lying down and kicking, rolling excessively, sweating profusely, etc.
2 When the temperature rises more than one degree above normal.
3 When the pulse reaches 50 beats per minute or more.
4 When blood from a wound cannot be stemmed, or is spurting in unison with the heart beat.
5 When the owner is in doubt about the seriousness of any injury or ailment.

The sick horse should be kept quiet and warm, and put on a laxative diet. The concentrate element in the diet must be reduced when the horse is off work. Failure to do this will result in further undesirable and dangerous complications.

Digestive Disorders
Loss of appetite (see also Chapter 3)
If a horse loses interest in his food it could mean that there is some underlying disorder. However, lack of appetite may also be a result of: poor quality, dirty or stale food; sharp teeth; a dirty manger or the presence of vermin; exhaustion; a change of routine; or bullying from the horse in the next stable. All these possibilities should be investigated thoroughly.

Colic
Colic is an uncomfortable and painful condition. It is at best unpleasant and at worst fatal. It is not a specific disease but a general term describing pain in the abdomen or other parts of the digestive system. It can be caused by an accumulation of gas in the gut, or by eating too much at one feed. It may result from excessive feeding before work or from drinking very cold water. Horses that eat the bedding are particularly prone to this

condition. Colic may also be caused by a twisting of the gut or by severe worm infestation.

The horse will show that he has pain in the abdomen in a number of ways. He may lie down and roll excessively, turn his head to bite the flank, kick at his belly with a hind leg and break out in a patchy sweat.

In all cases of colic where the pulse rate rises above 50, or the situation is not relieved in half an hour or so, the veterinary surgeon should be called. To make an inaccurate diagnosis and to administer the wrong treatment can be extremely dangerous.

The first treatment should be to alleviate the pain and to tranquillise the patient in a well padded, warm box. The horse should be kept warm with light rugs, but should these become wet with sweat they should be changed. Every effort should be made to prevent the horse from rolling violently as this may cause further damage. The traditional practice of walking the horse round constantly may tire him and lower his resistance, so it should therefore be used with caution.

A colic drink can be made up by the veterinary surgeon to be kept in the stable for use where mild cases of colic occur frequently. It should be used with care and only as first-aid treatment.

Many cases of colic are simply mild attacks of stomach ache, and after treatment will go away. It is important to watch that such cases do not reoccur too frequently, which would indicate that something is clearly wrong with the digestive system or the stable management.

The horse has a small stomach and is unable to vomit. This makes him particularly susceptible to any sort of pressure that builds up in the digestive system, especially the stomach. The treatment will depend on the diagnosis. Should the pain be caused by excessive gas pressure the veterinary surgeon may relieve this pressure with a stomach tube. Rectal examination will often disclose that the horse is constipated and manual removal of the faeces often relieves the condition. Enemas are used at times, and there are very effective drugs that can be used to relax the muscles and allow the normal functions of the digestive system to take place. In the worst cases, where colic is caused by a twisting or rupturing of the gut, surgery may be necessary.

Colic is a serious condition that can be found in the best run stables. It is sometimes, however, the result of carelessness, ignorance or both.

Infections
The horse owner is most likely to have to deal with infection in the following circumstances:

1 Infected wounds.
2 Skin diseases.
3 Respiratory conditions.

Serious infection of wounds can best be avoided by ensuring that the horse is regularly immunised against tetanus. This inoculation is given annually, and a booster is sometimes given where wounds are potentially susceptible to tetanus infection, for example injuries to the sole of the foot, or deep punctures elsewhere.

Other wounds should be kept clean and treated with an antibiotic powder to reduce the risk of bacterial infection (see page 96).

Skin Diseases
Lice
Lice are a common problem irritating the skin of neglected or ungroomed animals. They can be seen together with their eggs and cast-off skins in the mane and the base of the tail. They feed on the horse's blood causing itching, debility and loss of hair. Cure can be effected by sprinkling agricultural louse powder down the mane and along the back of the animal. This kills only the lice and not the eggs, so it is necessary to repeat the treatment over a period of several weeks. Where possible the horse should be clipped, the clippings burned and the horse's coat run over lightly with a singeing lamp.

Sweet itch
An allergic condition found in horses and ponies from June until about September, sweet itch is generally thought to be a reaction to the bite of a fly. The intense irritation causes the animal to rub its mane and tail, and unsightly, sore patches form. The veterinary surgeon will prescribe a solution to relieve this

condition. Horses and ponies that suffer from sweet itch (some do very much more than others) should, where possible, be kept in during the day and turned out at night during this period of the year. This usually gives some protection from the flies; the use of a strong fly repellent is also often helpful.

Ringworm
This highly contagious condition shows on the horse's coat as circular, raised patches about the size of a ten pence piece. The hair in the infected area falls away leaving a sore patch. A lotion is available with which the infected areas can be treated. The horse with ringworm should be isolated, grooming should be stopped and his rugs and grooming kit should be treated with a strong disinfectant. The bedding from his box should be burned. Feeding additives are available which can give the horse some immunity from this infection. They are particularly useful where the horse is unavoidably in contact with infected animals, in the hunting field for instance.

Contagious acne
This disease is sometimes confused with ringworm. Small, round, inflamed areas appear on the horse's coat usually in the girth and saddle area. This condition can be treated with tincture of iodine. It is highly contagious, which necessitates the isolation of the horse and disinfestation of all the tack, kit and equipment that has come into contact with him. Soiled bedding should be burned and not put on the muck heap.

Warbles
The eggs of the warble fly are laid on the horse's legs during the summer months. When the eggs hatch the minute larvae penetrate the skin and migrate up through the horse's body. They usually surface just under the skin in the saddle area of the back. Very often they bore through the skin to restart the life cycle. Sometimes the maggot dies just under the skin and requires surgical removal. This often leaves a persistent sore which prevents the horse being ridden for some time.

Respiratory Conditions

Equine influenza

This condition is generally known as 'the cough' because this is sometimes the only obvious symptom. It is highly infectious and can cause the horse to be off work for some weeks. The first sign is usually a slight fever that may go unnoticed, followed by a deep and often distressing cough. Caused by a virus, it often occurs between July and September. The treatment is to rest the horse and to put him on a laxative diet until the cough has completely gone. His return to full work should be slow and progressive. The veterinary surgeon should be called as antibiotic injections may be necessary to discourage secondary, bacterial infection. The risk of catching equine influenza can now be greatly reduced by immunisation. A highly efficient vaccine is available; at present two doses are given with an interval of six weeks between them, thereafter protection is given by a single dose once a year. Great care must be taken to ensure that the veterinary surgeon's advice is strictly carried out with regard to exercise in the period immediately following the inoculations. Entry to most horse shows and horse trials is now usually only available to those who can show certificates of immunisation against equine influenza for their horses.

Strangles

This highly infectious condition is caused by pus-forming organisms. The symptoms are fever, lassitude and lack of interest in food. A thick nasal discharge appears and the glands at the angles of the lower jaw swell, causing difficulty in swallowing. The infected horse must be isolated immediately and the veterinary surgeon must be called. Soft, moist mashes should be given to tempt the horse to eat. Feeding utensils and grooming kit should be disinfected twice a day and soiled bedding must be burned. Only one person should deal with the horse; overalls and boots should be worn, and left in the stable where the infected horse is kept. They should be disinfected regularly.

The swollen glands may be bathed with a warm solution of Epsom salts to bring the swelling to a head ready for lancing. Once the swellings of the glands have burst or have been lanced the condition usually improves, but the horse will require careful sick nursing (see page 94).

The common cold

The equine cold is very similar to the human cold. It starts with a rise in temperature, lassitude and a runny nose, and is very infectious. Treatment consists of taking the patient off all work, and keeping him warm with plenty of fresh air but no draughts. He should be on a daily diet of warm, moist bran mashes. The doors and windows should be open once a day and he should be thoroughly groomed without being allowed to get cold.

The cold will run its course in about ten days, but a recovery period of about a month is required to bring the horse gradually back into work. The cold is usually accompanied by a cough. No attempt should be made to bring the horse back into work whilst he is still coughing. The symptoms can be relieved by applying an electuary to the back of the tongue or by steaming the horse's head (see page 98).

Emphysema

This condition is rather like 'farmer's lung' in the human. Spores from hay and straw are breathed into the lungs causing irritation and a very dry cough. It is not 'broken wind' and is, in most cases, curable. To relieve this condition the horse must be kept in a dust-free environment. All his feeds should be damp and his hay should be soaked in water overnight. As an alternative to hay, one of the vacuum-packed, dried grass products may be used (see Chapter 3).

Horses suffering from emphysematous conditions (see page 41) should be bedded down on wood shavings or peat, to avoid subjecting them to the spores that are found in straw. An electuary sometimes brings relief when the horse is coughing. Work should be regulated to avoid too much hard galloping in dry, dusty conditions. A short pipe opener, once a week, may however help a horse that suffers in this way.

Lameness

Lameness is probably the most common veterinary problem with which the horse owner is confronted. The possibility of the horse going lame increases with the speed at which he is required to work and with the demands of competition riding.

There are many reasons for a horse becoming lame: an injury, disease, immaturity, old age, or heredity. Some lameness is

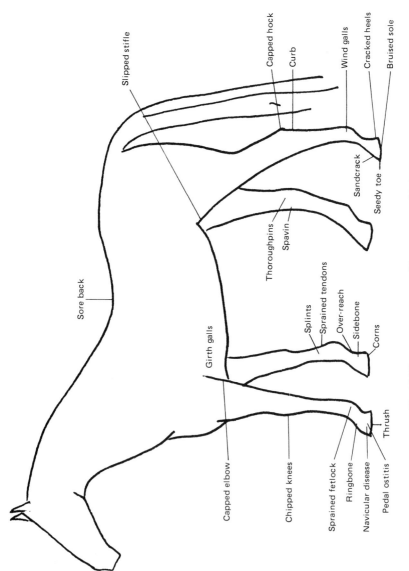

Fig 12 The common seats of lameness and injury

peculiar to certain types of horse and the work that they are required to do. A major cause of lameness is the horse being asked to carry out activities for which he has not been sufficiently well prepared.

Lameness is manifested by the horse in his stance or gait. In severe cases he may, whilst standing still, rest a leg or even hold it entirely off the ground. The lameness may show in walk but it is usually most easily seen when the horse is trotting.

Foreleg lameness is most easily seen as the horse is trotted towards one. As the lame leg comes to the ground he will lift his head up in an effort to take weight off that leg. As the sound leg comes to the ground he will lower his head again. Hind leg lameness is best seen as the horse is trotted away. The hind quarter on the lame side will be raised as the foot or leg that is in pain is on the ground. The quarter will be lowered as the sound leg is on the ground.

Difficulty arises when the horse is lame in both forelegs, or diagonally lame, for instance in the left foreleg and the right hand leg. In principle he will try to reduce the weight that the painful limb, or limbs, are bearing.

Having identified the limb in which the horse is lame, the seat of lameness must then be established. This is usually shown by the presence of a wound, heat, pain, swelling or a combination of two or more of these symptoms. Infection is at times identified by smell, as with thrush for instance. Where none of these symptoms is present, deep examination will probably be required. X-ray or nerve blocking can be used, both of which require professional attention.

The chances of avoiding lameness are increased by:

1 Meticulous daily care of the feet. Regular picking out. Care of the frog, sole and walls of the hoof.
2 Careful, regular and correct shoeing.
3 Progressive training and preparation for hunting or competition riding.
4 Feeding the correct diet.
5 Good stable management.
6 Fitting the horse with protective boots or bandages when required.
7 Avoiding work on very hard or very wet ground.

The foot

Lameness is most often caused by problems in the foot. The sole and the frog are very vulnerable to puncture wounds which can cause infection. This in turn brings heat and swelling, causing pain in the confined area within the hoof.

Pus in the foot This is a major cause of lameness and can arise from the infection of any foot injury. Its presence can often be established by manual examination. Pressing hard with the fingers on the sole, frog, bulbs of the heels or the coronet, or tapping the wall of the hoof lightly with a hammer, may result in the horse flinching when the painful area is touched. This examination, palpation as it is called, should be carried out with care, especially when severe pain is expected. Pus may be dispersed with anti-biotics. It may also be drained by a veterinary surgeon or skilled farrier by surgical means. This course should never be undertaken by the unskilled. Relief of pain can be obtained by poulticing (see page 97) or tubbing (see page 98) the foot. This treatment causes the abscess to mature and burst, sometimes through the coronet.

Laminitis This condition, which is more likely to affect ponies than horses, is caused by over-feeding or a pony being allowed too much rich, spring grass. This results in the inflammation and swelling of the sensitive laminae within the feet causing great pressure and pain. The condition occurs mainly in the forefeet. The animal will be reluctant to move and in severe cases will stand on his heels, with the forelegs stretched out in front in an attempt to take the weight off the feet. Laminitis can be treated successfully by immediate veterinary attention but if left it will almost certainly result in irreversible damage. Temporary relief can be given to the animal by cold hosing the feet or standing him in a cool running stream.

Navicular disease This condition sometimes arises in the horse at about seven years of age. It is the deterioration of a small bone deep in the foot called the navicular bone. The reasons for its deterioration are not yet entirely agreed by the veterinary profession but various treatments do exist to relieve its effects. The onset of navicular disease is usually shown by a rather pottery stride, and lameness may come and go in the early stages. Both forefeet are usally affected although the symptoms may show rather more in one than the other. X-ray of the feet may be required to confirm the presence of navicular disease.

Upright, boxy feet with contracted heels and steep pasterns are more prone to this disease than are feet with better conformation. It is probably due to the increased concussion on the foot, caused by this upright conformation, that this disease is encouraged.

Whilst modern pain-killers reduce the effect of navicular disease, the morality of their use must be questionable. Certainly the horse in which navicular disease is confirmed is finished as a reliable competition horse. His future as a riding horse must, at least, be suspect.

Ringbone Ringbone is an arthritic condition causing pain in the foot or lower part of the leg. Where it occurs between the long and the short pastern bones it is known as 'high' ringbone and where it occurs between the short pastern bone and the pedal bone it is called 'low' ringbone. These conditions are also sometimes known as 'true' or 'false' ringbone. Its presence can be felt around these joints as a bony growth at the front and sides of the pastern bone. With a mild form the horse can continue in work to a degree depending on the severity of the condition. Ringbone however will most likely preclude the horse from any serious competition work.

Corns These are found on the underside of the foot, usually at 'the seat of corn' (see Plate 29). They are caused by sustained or repeated pressure, often from an ill-fitting shoe, which bruises the sensitive part of the foot. The corn can be cut out by the veterinary surgeon or the farrier. The hole is plugged and the horse fitted with a corn shoe designed to take the pressure off the seat of corn.

Thrush This is an infection of the foot found in and around the cleft of the frog. It is generally accepted to be caused by neglect and poor stable management, and is the result of allowing organic matter to build up and remain in the areas of the foot that are abnormally deprived of ventilation and fresh air. The decomposition of this organic matter causes infection, and a foul condition and smell become present in the foot. The horse's feet should be thoroughly picked out at least once a day when he is kept at grass and three or four times a day when stabled. When thrush is found, the foot should be thoroughly picked out, and scrubbed with soap and water. It must then be completely dried and dressed with an antiseptic astringent such as Stockholm tar or creosote. Mild thrush is unlikely to cause lameness, but if it is allowed to become a chronic condition, lameness may well occur.

Pedal ostitis (inflammation of the pedal bone) Pedal ostitis is usually caused by repeated concussion. It may occur in both forefeet but usually only one is involved. The symptoms are similar to those of navicular disease: there is a pottery action and lameness, which goes when the horse is rested. It is generally thought to be incurable but expert shoeing and careful use may keep the sufferer in modest work.

Bruised sole Some horses have particularly thin soles and are, consequently, prone to this injury. It is, however, not confined to thin soled horses and is usually caused by treading on a stone or some other hard object. Rest is the most effective treatment, sometimes helped by tubbing the foot. Horses that suffer persistently from bruising of the sole can be protected by having a leather pad fitted under the shoe to cover the sole, or by wearing boots that protect the sole.

Sidebones These are caused by the ossification of the lateral cartilages which are two wings of cartilage either side of the foot about level with the coronary band and just in front of the bulbs of the heels. In a young horse this would be considered to be an unsoundness as it may suggest a tendency to form new bone together with the lameness that it may cause. It is less serious in older horses in that in time all cartilage tends to ossify and once the ossification is complete the horse will usually work sound.

Seedy toe This is a separation of the horn of the foot from the sensitive, underlying tissues. It can appear in any part of the hoof but is usually at the toe. It is sometimes caused, and certainly aggravated, by grit or dirt being forced up into the gap between the horn and the underlying tissue. It is usually the result of pressure or careless shoeing, but at times the cause is difficult to identify. The cure must be effected by the vet and the blacksmith.

Sandcrack This is a crack that appears in the hoof starting at the coronet and extending down the wall of the hoof to some degree. It is usually caused by injury to the coronet or something that interferes with the proper nutrition of the horn. Veterinary advice should be sought for horses suffering from this condition.

Grass cracks These appear in the wall of the hoof starting at the bottom and working up towards the coronet. They are usually caused by injury to the horn and are generally found in unshod animals. Poor nutrition of the horn and neglect of the feet may contribute to this condition. Treatment consists of the removal of the causes and the blacksmith burning a groove in the horn at the top of the crack to discourage its progress up the hoof.

The leg
The fetlock joint Often found to be a seat of lameness, this joint is put under great strain when the horse jumps, canters fast or gallops. In such work there are regular periods when the entire weight of both horse and rider is supported on one leg. Hard going increases the effects of concussion and deep, wet going increases the wrenching effect on the joint. This may result in the straining of the fetlock joint, where heat, pain and swelling may be present, or where puffy enlargements, known as 'wind galls', may appear.

A mild strain of the fetlock joint usually responds to rest, cold hosing or poulticing. Persistent or severe lameness in this area requires veterinary attention.

Damage to the sesamoid bones, or the sheathes surrounding them (sesamoiditis), the suspensory ligament, or the tendons in this area, requires rest and veterinary treatment.

Splints These are small, hard lumps of bone appearing on the splint bones, which are the vestigial remains of two toes that lie either side of the cannon bone. Splints do not necessarily cause lameness, and once they are hardened, whilst unsightly, they do not usually cause any trouble, especially when they are on the

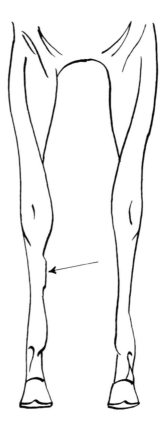

Fig 13 The splint, formed on the side of the cannon bone

side of the cannon bone. If, however, they form at the back of the cannon bone and interfere with the back tendons, surgery may be necessary to remove them. Rest is usually sufficient to overcome this problem in most cases, and a mild, working blister may assist the healing process.

The most common cause of splints is the galloping and jumping of young horses before they are capable of coping with strenuous work.

Tendons and ligaments The suspension and locomotion of the horse depend upon a series of tendons and ligaments. In the horse's natural state this suspensory system is very efficient. When the horse is domesticated and put under the strains of competition riding or hunting the system frequently breaks down.

Tendons are the strong bands of sinew that operate the joints by the action of the muscles. Ligaments are the strong bands of fibre that hold the joints together. Both these types of fibrous bands can be strained with various degrees of severity. Such strains always require veterinary attention. There are many sophisticated veterinary techniques for the repair of strained tendons and ligaments, but there is only one really effective remedy and that is rest. One year's rest in the case of a severe strain may show some improvement but two years is far more likely to give lasting results. Prevention is much better than cure, and the possibility of tendon strain can be reduced to the minimum by careful preparation and training and the avoidance of very hard or very deep going.

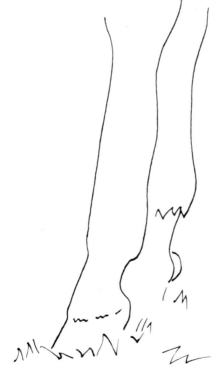

Fig 14 A 'bowed' tendon on the near fore

The knee This is a complicated joint and whilst it is prone to the effects of concussion most injuries to the knee are caused by falls. The condition known as 'chipped knees' arises from the horse slipping or stumbling on to his knees causing injury and unsightly, lasting scars. These scars may mean that the animal is prone to stumbling, which is a fault in some horses. Any injury to a joint that involves the loss of 'joint oil' is serious and requires veterinary attention. Puncture wounds to the knee can be serious and require professional treatment.

The elbow Lameness in the elbow is rare and is usually caused by direct, external injury. An unsightly condition known as 'capped elbow' occurs at times. This is a bursal enlargement around the point of the elbow caused by insufficient stable bedding, or by the heels of the fore shoe coming in contact with the elbow when the horse lies down. The fitting of a 'sausage boot' around the pastern at night may help to prevent this injury.

The shoulders Lameness in this area is rare but may occur if a muscle involved in the articulation of the shoulder is damaged. Rest is probably the best remedy but veterinary advice should be sought.

The stifle joint The stifle is the equivalent to the human knee joint and has a patalla or knee cap. The condition known as a 'slipped stifle' is not uncommon and occurs when the horse's hind leg is fully extended behind. It causes a locking of the patella and prevents the horse returning his hind leg to its normal position. The condition can be rectified with veterinary help but repeated slipping of the stifle can result in permanent damage.

The hock This large, complicated and important joint is put under great strain in the competition horse when he is jumping, galloping or making turns at speed. The hock is prone to arthritic changes, the best known being the so-called 'spavins'. These are either 'bone' or 'bog' spavins. The bone spavin is a hard swelling on the inside of the front of the hock caused by the growth of new bone. The bog spavin is the result of an inflamed joint producing more joint oil which causes bulges at three different places: one on the inside of the front of the hock and the other two, on either

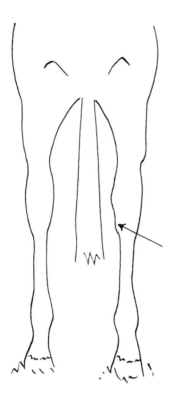

Fig 15 A good hock (left); a 'spavined' hock (right)

side, higher up the joint. These are serious causes of lameness and seldom respond well to treatment.

The capped hock is an unsightly bursal enlargement at the point of the hock. It is caused by insufficient or unsuitable stable bedding. It is unlikely to cause lameness.

The curb This is an unsoundness which shows as a swelling on the back of the cannon about a hand's breadth below the point of the hock (see Fig 16). It is caused by overwork, particularly in young horses where the tendon that runs down the back of the cannon bone from the point of the hock has been strained. At first the horse may be lame but after about two to three weeks he should be sound and very light work can by resumed. Cold hosing helps but blistering should be avoided. Normal work can be resumed in about three months but strain should always be avoided. A curb

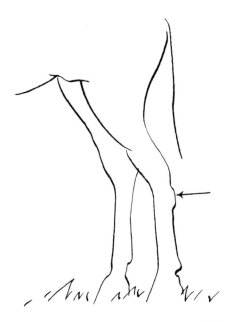

Fig 16 The curb, seen clearly just below the hock

is a sign of weak hocks and horses showing a tendency towards curbs should be avoided for competition work.

Thoroughpin This is an unsightly blemish in the hock joint. Whilst it is unlikely to cause lameness it may indicate a weakness in the hock. It is a distention of the sheath of the deep flexor tendon where it passes over the arch of the hock. It shows as swellings on both sides of the joint about level with the point of the hock. Pressure on one swelling will push the sinovial fluid causing the swelling to move from one side of the joint to the other. Various treatments are available, but are not as a rule lasting.

Cracked heels and grease These two separate conditions result in sore patches forming in the hollow of the heel and at the back of the pastern. Usually caused by the horse standing in damp cold conditions or by careless washing of the legs, the affected areas become chapped and sore, causing lameness in severe cases. The affected areas should be kept clean and dry. Veterinary advice should be sought.

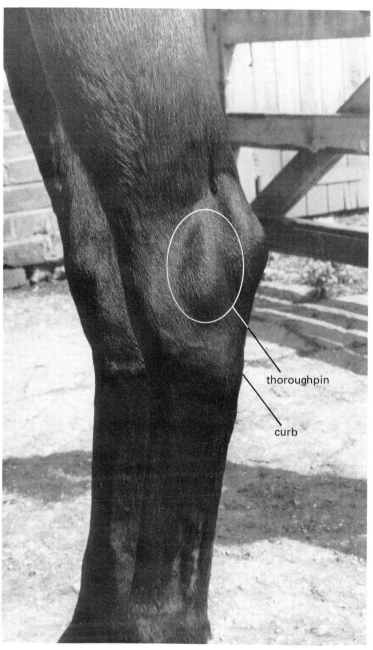

thoroughpin

curb

Plate 28 A spectacular thoroughpin and curby hocks

Minor Injuries

Girth galls
These occur where an ill-fitting or loose girth rubs the horse's side. They may occur in soft, fat animals just up from grass. The injured area should be treated with a saline solution or an anti-biotic powder. To prevent repetition the girth must be kept clean and soft, and should fit the horse without pinching or rubbing and with the underlying skin being flat and free from wrinkles. The area in which girth galls are likely to occur can be hardened by the topical application of methylated spirit. The horse should not be saddled again until the girth galls are quite healed.

Sore back
This is sometimes caused by a dirty or ill-fitting saddle or numnah. It may, on occasions, be caused by bad riding. The treatment and prevention is the same as for girth galls with particular care that both the saddle and numnah, if used, fit correctly.

Over-reach
This injury occurs when the heels of the forefeet are struck by the toes of the hind feet. There are a number of reasons for this but it usually happens when horses are ridden too fast and out of control, or when the tired horse is galloped through deep or difficult going. It is of course also sustained as an accident when none of these conditions is responsible. Prevention is best achieved by avoiding these circumstances. Surgical shoeing may help and the fitting of over-reach boots is very effective (see pages 138–9).

Treatment of an over-reach is the same as for any contused wound (see page 96).

Internal Parasites
All horses suffer from internal parasites to a degree. In order to keep the infestation to a minimum, and so to have a healthy and economically kept horse, regular precautions must be taken. These precautions are divided into two areas: care of the pasture; care of the horse.

Good grassland management is the first stage in controlling horse parasites as the worm larvae are ingested by the horse on infected grass (see Chapter 2).

The effect of an infestation of internal parasites in the horse can be very serious. At best it can cause discomfort for the horse and expense to the owner, at worst it can cause death. Foals and young horses are particularly at risk. In order to keep internal parasites to the minimum the horse must be dosed regularly with a 'wormer'. This is a chemical which can be administered by any horse owner. It breaks into the life cycle of the parasite whilst it is in the horse and so reduces the effects of the worm and prevents it completing its life cycle. There are many brands of wormer on the market; all are given orally either in the food or by syringe into the horse's mouth. It is recommended that patent wormers are changed from time to time, as some parasites may develop an immunity to a particular brand.

The veterinary surgeon can make tests to assess the degree of infestation from which a horse may be suffering and consequently prescribe the treatment. It is usually an advantage to seek his advice in the first instance.

Horses may be infected with four types of worms: the large red worm; the small red worm; the pin worm or seat worm; the lung worm.

The large red worm
The most serious of the internal parasites, the large red worm is thought to be the most common cause of recurrent, spasmodic colic. Apart from causing death in apparently healthy horses it can also cause delibity and 'poor doing' . The symptoms of infestation with this worm are loss of weight, a dull coat and diarrhoea. Some adult horses can carry heavy worm infestations without showing any symptoms.

The small red worm
This is usually found in the horse together with the large red worm. Its life cycle is different and it causes massive ulceration and inflammation of the wall of the large intestine if it is not controlled. The symptoms of small red worm infestation are scouring, which at times alternates with constipation, poor condition and anaemia.

Seat worm or pin worm
The adult worms inhabit the horse's large intestine and the female passes partially out of the rectum to lay eggs on the skin surrounding the anus. The larvae drop from the eggs to infect the grass and continue the worm's life cycle.

The intense itching caused by the females laying their eggs on the skin compels the horse to rub his tail against a fence post or a wall, making an unsightly and uncomfortable sore at the top of the tail. The condition is easy to identify as clusters of cream-coloured eggs can be seen around the anus.

Lung worm
Donkeys carry lung worm and it does not seem to affect them adversely. However, it can cause serious lung problems in the horse and consequently coughing. It is not easy to diagnose in horses and is usually only discovered by a process of elimination. Horses should not be kept in fields with donkeys or in fields in which donkeys have recently been grazing.

Bots
These are the larvae of the gadfly which can infect the horse. The gadfly lays its eggs on the horse, often on the forelegs where the horse can lick them off. They can be seen as small yellow eggs about an eighth of an inch long. The larvae burrow into the lips, gums and tongue of the horse and later migrate to the stomach from which they are passed out in the dung to restart their life cycle.

Bot infestation may cause loss of condition, staring coat, rise in temperature, quickened pulse, intermittent constipation and diarrhoea.

Sick Nursing
Efficient and considerate nursing is an important part of treating the sick or recuperating horse. Without good nursing his recovery may be delayed or even prevented.

The sick horse should be kept in a well-ventilated, but draught-free, loose box, as far as possible away from other horses and from noise and other activities. The bed should be deep and comfortable, and made from short straw to enable the horse to move around without great effort.

The patient should be kept warm with light woollen rugs loosely fitted. The legs can be bandaged with woollen stable bandages and where necessary a hood can be worn. Massage of the legs and ears is comforting to a sick horse; it helps with the circulation and the maintenance of the body temperature. If the stable is heated artificially it must not be at the expense of good ventilation. The fire hazard caused by some means of artificial heating must also be considered. Unless it is expressly forbidden by the veterinary surgeon an easily accessible supply of drinking water must be provided.

Sick horses are frequently off their feed. They should be offered fresh green food, eggs, stout, milk or any succulent food that may tempt them to eat. Uneaten food should not be left in the box for long periods, and no attempt should be made to force the horse to eat.

Vigorous grooming should be avoided; cleaning off night stains, picking out the feet and washing the eyes, nose and dock should be sufficient. The rugs must be taken off and shaken daily but the horse must not be left entirely uncovered at any time.

When treatment and medicine are prescribed by the veterinary surgeon they must be meticulously administered in accordance with his instructions. It is sometimes necessary to keep records of the patient's pulse, temperature and respiration.

The very sick horse should never be left entirely alone. He will do better with some human company and someone should always be in attendance in case of emergency.

If the horse is likely to be off the road for more than a day or two the shoes should be removed. As the horse recovers it will be necessary to lead him out for very short periods, only a few yards to start with, perhaps for a few minutes in hand for a little grass. His reintroduction to work must be in accordance with the veterinary surgeon's instructions. The return to the normal diet should be made gradually.

In the circumstances where the sick horse is suffering from a contagious or infectious disease he must be isolated from other horses to reduce the possibility of the infection being spread. It is a useful precaution if his attendant is kept away from other horses whilst the risk of infection lasts. If this is not convenient other strict isolation measures must be carried out:

1 The infected horse must have his own grooming kit, feed bowl, water bucket, rugs etc, which are not allowed to come into contact with other horses.
2 The person attending the sick horse must keep overalls, boots and rubber gloves at the isolation stable and these should not be allowed to come into contact with other horses.
3 A bowl of disinfectant, soap, scrubbing brush and a towel must be kept at the isolation box for the use of the veterinary surgeon and the attendant after each visit to the sick horse.
4 Stable bedding and muck that are removed from the isolation box should be burned and not put on the muck heap.
5 When the horse has recovered, all the items of clothing, including the headcollar, and bandages that have been used on him should be disinfected. The stable must be emptied and thoroughly scrubbed out with a strong disinfectant.

First-aid Treatment

The horse owner must not attempt to be his own veterinary surgeon. There are however some first-aid skills and nursing practices that should be developed by those who look after horses.

Wounds

Wounds fall generally into three groups:

1 Incised wounds. Cuts made by a knife, a tin or a piece of glass.
2 Tears. Wounds made by barbed wire or jagged metal.
3 Punctures. Penetrating wounds like those made by a nail in the foot or a thorn in the knee.

In the case of incised wounds and tears, stem the bleeding by applying a pad of gauze, or any other clean material, directly onto the wound and hold it there until the bleeding stops. Clean the wound thoroughly with salt water (one teaspoonful of salt to 600ml (1 pint) of warm water); do not use antiseptics, disinfectants or detergents. Apply an anti-biotic powder. The wound may need to be stitched, which will require the services of a veterinary surgeon. An anti-tetanus injection may be required.

In the case of puncture wounds, stem the bleeding and dress the wound with an anti-biotic powder. In order to remove infection from this type of wound it may be necessary to apply a poultice. Such wounds are particularly dangerous due to the possibility of tetanus.

Poultices
These can be applied to relieve pain, heat and swelling, and to draw infection from a wound, on any part of the horse's body to which they can be safely attached. A poultice can be made from kaolin paste, bran or a patent impregnated gamgee such as 'Animalintex'.

A kaolin poultice is suitable to apply to a leg where there is heat or swelling, for instance in the fetlock joint or the back tendons. The kaolin paste is heated in its tin, with the lid off, until it is hotter than can be borne on the hand. The paste is then spread with a knife onto a piece of gamgee cut sufficiently large to cover the area that is to be treated. (The paste should be a little over an eighth of an inch thick on the gamgee.) It is then applied with the kaolin paste towards the leg, covered with some waterproof material and secured with a stable bandage. The poultice must not be allowed to dry out and should be changed every twenty-four hours.

'Animalintex' is a very useful poultice which consists of gamgee that is ready treated. It has to be soaked in boiling water and when it is of a suitable temperature, it is applied in the same way as the kaolin poultice.

A bran poultice is suitable to apply to the sole of the foot. First the leg should be bandaged from below the knee down to the fetlock joint, and the heel smeared with grease to prevent chapping. A small bran mash should then be made to which has been added a handful of Epsom salts and some non-irritant antiseptic. The mash is put, hot, into a strong plastic bag and the affected foot put into the bag so that there is about two inches of bran under the sole. The foot and the dressing should then, ideally, be put into a poultice boot. If this is not available the foot can be put into the corner of a sack which is secured around the leg with a second bandage, the surplus sacking being removed with scissors. Whilst this poultice is in place the horse should be kept on a short rack, ie tied up so that he cannot bite at the dressing or walk around too much. The poultice should be renewed twice a day.

In the circumstances where one foreleg is being treated and

there is a possibility that extra weight will be supported on the sound leg, it is a useful precaution to fit a support bandage to the sound leg.

Tubbing

This is a method of applying a type of poultice to the foot, particularly the sole, where it will have a drawing effect on injuries. A wooden or strong plastic bucket should be used, about one-third filled with warm to fairly hot water, to which a handful of Epsom salts is added.

The foot is put carefully into the bucket, and kept there for ten to fifteen minutes. Cold water can be used to reduce pain and swelling, but it is more effective to stand the horse in a cold, running stream where possible. Tubbing should be carried out twice a day until relief is obtained.

Cold water treatment

Pain, heat and swelling can sometimes be relieved by the application of cold water. This can be done in a number of ways.

Where the feet or the fetlock joints have to be treated, as in the case of laminitis or strained fetlocks, it is useful to be able to stand the horse in a cold, running stream for twenty minutes or so. For the treatment of the forearm, knees or tendons, running cold water from a hose over the injured area for twenty minutes two or three times a day will often be very effective.

In circumstances where neither of these practices is possible, cold water bandages can be used, being changed every half an hour or so. (The application of a hot bandage is often useful too; the water should be as hot as the hand can bear.)

Steaming

Nasal congestion can be relieved by steaming. A handful of hay is put into the corner of a sack and a teaspoonful of Friar's balsam or oil of eucalyptus is added to it. Enough boiling water is then added to make an inhalant and the sack is held over the horse's nose while he is encouraged to inhale the fumes.

The veterinary first-aid cabinet

Veterinary first-aid equipment should be kept in all well-run stables. It is unnecessary, and usually wasteful, to keep large stocks but the following list will provide adequate cover in case of emergency:

7.5cm (3in) cotton bandages × 4.
7.5cm (3in) support bandages × 2.
Gamgee 1 roll.
Medical gauze 1 roll.
Cotton wool 1 large roll.
Surgical lint 1 roll.
7.5cm (3in) adhesive tape 1 roll.
Wound powder, usually in a plastic puffer bottle.
Anti-biotic aerosol spray.
Colic drink. This can be provided by the veterinary surgeon, together with directions for its use.
Epsom salts 225g (8oz) packet.
Common salt 225g (8oz) packet.
Vaseline, a small jar.
Kaolin, or some other type of poultice.
Scissors with round ends.
Clinical thermometer.

The quantity of each item that is stocked depends on the number of horses that are kept in the stable, and the type of work on which they are employed. Other items such as cough electuary, Friar's balsam and amoricaine powder tend to deteriorate and are best purchased as and when they are required.

These items should be kept in an easily accessible but secure place, and, of course, in hygienic conditions. It is helpful to keep the telephone number and address of the local veterinary surgeon on, or in, the first-aid cabinet.

Shoeing

In his natural environment, on soft grassy plains, the horse's foot serves him well. It grows sufficiently to replace the horn worn down by daily wear and tear and provides enough grip for him to move about quite freely at all his natural paces. When he is domesticated and trained as a riding or draught horse, he is subjected to unnatural strains which, without precautions being taken, will result in damage to the foot and possibly other parts of the body. Shoeing was first practised by the Romans some two thousand years ago. Whilst many attempts have been made to improve on this practice over the years, none has been successful. Today the principle of shoeing the horse is little changed from Roman times.

The horse is shod for three basic reasons:

1 To protect the foot from the unnatural wear and tear put upon it when the horse is ridden.
2 To improve the grip on the ground, rather like running spikes or the studs in football boots.
3 For surgical reasons. The skilled farrier, in conjunction with the veterinary surgeon, can shoe the horse to relieve some injuries or deformities that would otherwise detract from his usefulness.

All farriers are required to serve a four-year apprenticeship and to pass an examination for the Diploma of the Worshipful Company of Farriers. Shoeing horses is an extremely skilled craft and should be attempted only by those who are experienced and qualified. A well-shod horse is the result of co-operation between the farrier, who brings his skill, and the owner, who trains the horse to stand quietly whilst being shod, and provides a clean, well-lit area in which the farrier can work.

Horses usually need shoeing about every four to six weeks. If at the end of this time the shoe is not worn out the horse will almost certainly require a 'remove', ie the shoe removed, the foot trimmed back and the old shoe replaced. A horse needs to be shod if the shoe is worn out or loose; the clenches have risen; the foot has grown too long; the shoe has sprung or twisted.

A well-shod foot will show the following characteristics:

1 The shoe must be the correct design and the appropriate weight for the animal.
2 The shoe must be made to fit the foot. The foot must never be rasped down to fit the shoe. This is called 'dumping' and is a sign of really bad workmanship. None of the sole may be cut away by the farrier, or any of the frog other than the part which is really rotten or hanging off.

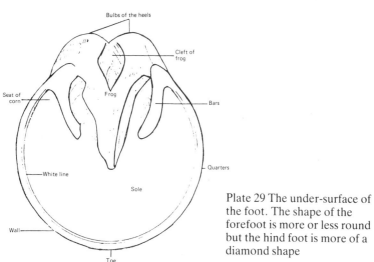

Bulbs of the heels

Cleft of
frog

Seat of
corn

Frog

Bars

White line

Quarters

Sole

Wall

Toe

Plate 29 The under-surface of
the foot. The shape of the
forefoot is more or less round
but the hind foot is more of a
diamond shape

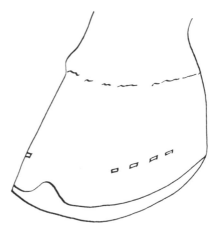

Fig 17 A well-shod foot

3 The heels of the shoes must be neither too long nor too short: too long and they risk being trodden on and pulled off; too short and the bearing surface of the foot on the shoe is reduced, with the possibility that corns will be made by the heels of the shoes digging into the 'seat of corn'.
4 The feet should be level.
5 Clean nail holes, evenly spaced between the toes and the quarters, should emerge in a straight line a third of the way up the wall of the hoof. There are usually three nails on the inside and four on the outside. They should be turned into strong clenches and rasped smooth.

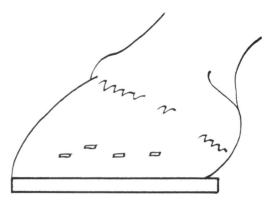

Fig 18 A poorly-shod foot: the toe has been 'dumped'; the heels are too long and not bevelled; the clenches are irregular

6 The bearing surface must be regular between the foot and the shoe, ie no daylight should show between the two.

7 Toe clips on the fore shoe and quarter clips on the hind shoe should be bedded into the wall and fit flush. The shoe should appear to be a regular extension of the foot.

8 Above all, the comfort and natural movement of the horse are paramount. The shoe is fitted to make his life easier and must never pinch or cause discomfort.

Horse shoes come in many different shapes and sizes, designed to suit a variety of animals and the various types of work that they are required to do.

Normally the hunter, the child's pony, the hack and the competition horse are fitted with the 'hunter' shoe. This is a fairly lightweight shoe made from fullered iron to improve the grip.

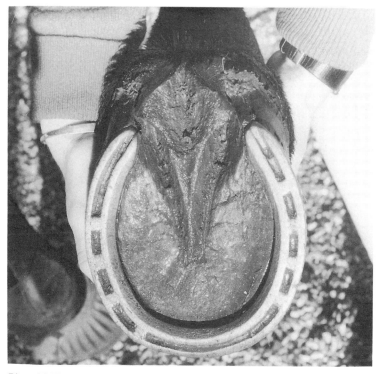

Plate 30 The fullered hunter fore shoe with pencilled heels and tapped for studs

The hind shoe may be fitted with a 'wedge heel and calkin' which help the horse to keep his footing. Modern shoes are usually machine made and are adjusted by the farrier to fit the individual horse. Most skilled farriers are, however, capable of making a set of shoes from the basic iron bar. 'Hot' shoeing is to be preferred to 'cold' shoeing as it gives the farrier much more opportunity to adjust the size of the shoe and to burn it onto the foot thereby ensuring that it is well seated.

Various studs can be fitted to the horse shoe to improve the grip for competition riding. The farrier should be notified if the shoes are required to be 'tapped' for screw-in studs (see Plate 30). A small permanent stud of the 'Mordax' variety can be fitted to the shoe, which is useful when the horse is required to work a lot on the road.

Grooming

Grooming is a vital part of the horse's daily care. It is required both by stabled horses and those kept at grass. Broadly, it can be divided into four areas: grooming the stabled horse; strapping; quartering; grooming the grass-kept horse.

Good grooming is a skill that requires practice and understanding, and it is required for a number of reasons:

1 To keep the horse clean and to remove waste products from the coat and skin.
2 To stimulate the circulation of the blood and lymph and improve the muscle tone.
3 To promote health and to discourage disease and infection.
4 To improve the appearance of the horse.
5 To ensure that the horse is inspected thoroughly, at least once a day.

Grooming the stabled horse

This should take an experienced groom about forty-five minutes, and done correctly it requires the groom to be fit, strong and agile. The horse should enjoy his grooming and co-operate with the groom. When the weather permits it adds to the enjoyment of both horse and groom if it can be done outside in the sun. The horse can be tied to a ring in the yard wall or to a fence rail and perhaps be given a hay net.

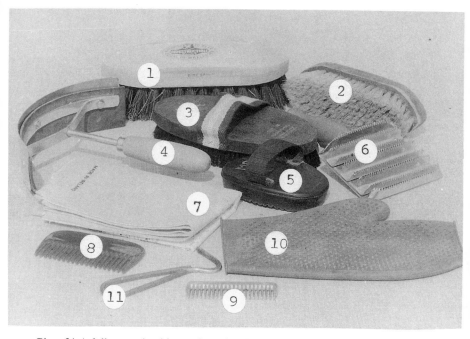

Plate 31 A full grooming kit consists of: 1 dandy brush for removing caked mud and dirt; 2 water brush for laying the mane and tail; 3 body brush for brushing the body, head and legs; 4 sweat scraper for removing moisture; 5 rubber curry comb for loosening scurf and dirt; 6 metal curry comb for cleaning the body brush; 7 stable rubber for a final polish; 8 mane comb; 9 pulling comb for pulling the mane and tail; 10 rubber grooming mit for massage; 11 hoof pick

Whether inside or out, a clean area is required in which to work. A muddy field is unsatisfactory for grooming as is a dirty loose box. The bedding should be put up to one side and the floor swept clean. The groom should wear a shirt, slacks and sensible boots or shoes. Too many clothes and soft shoes are an obvious disadvantage.

The good groom works in a quiet, confident way, encouraging the horse to be calm and relaxed. Timid or nervous horse handlers tend to make horses nervous too whilst the quiet, confident groom encourages similar qualities in the horse. Shouting and bullying on the part of the groom usually indicate that he is frightened.

Domesticated horses are normally quiet and accept human company but they depend on their speed and quick reactions for

Plate 32 When in a crouching position the groom can move away fairly easily in an emergency

Plate 33 In this position the groom is putting herself in some danger should the horse be startled

Plate 34 Picking out a forefoot

Plate 35 Picking out a hind foot

their defence. It is important to warn a horse of ones approach by speaking softly and to avoid taking him by surprise. The horse may, unintentionally, tread on his handler or shy into him when startled. It is therefore necessary for the groom to remain in a balanced position, able to move easily, when he is working on his horse (see Plate 32).

Grooming should be started by picking out the feet. If this is done in the same sequence each day, the horse will learn to pick up each foot in sequence as the groom requests. If the horse, initially, is not this co-operative the groom should start with a foreleg, putting a hand on the horse's shoulder and running it down the shoulder over the elbow and down the back of the leg, taking hold of the tuft of hair at the ergot or the fetlock joint; at the same time the horse must be asked to lift his foot. This should be done with the hand nearest the horse, the groom facing the rear. If the horse fails to lift his foot the groom can lean against the horse's shoulder, which often helps. The foot is lifted forward as it is raised and the horse should be given time to rebalance himself on three legs before work is started on the foot. To lift the hind foot, the groom, without taking the horse by surprise, should run a hand over the quarter and down the back of the leg over the hock to the fetlock joint. He should ask the horse to lift his foot as he takes it up to the rear.

The hoof pick must be used from the heel to the toe and with care. All dirt and dung must be removed to prevent the formation of thrush. The feet should, once or twice a week, be scrubbed out with warm, soapy water and a stiff brush. Care must be taken not to let water drain back into the heels or the back of the pastern as this may cause chapped or cracked heels. The foot must then be thoroughly dried and the sole and frog painted with a mild creosote solution to discourage infection. Whilst picking out the feet, the shoes, clenches, heels and coronet should be inspected.

Heavy night stains can then be removed from the body and the legs with the dandy brush. This brush must not be used on the head, the mane or the tail.

The next stage is to use the body brush vigorously all over the horse in small circles against the lie of the coat. This should be started on the near side, up behind the horse's ears. With the body brush held in the right hand and the metal curry comb in the left, the whole side of the horse is covered: down the neck, over the shoulder, down the foreleg, over the back, barrel, loins, hips, stifle, gaskin, hock and inside the thigh. Care should be taken around the sternum, belly, sheath or udder as these are ticklish areas. When the whole of the near side has been completed the coat should then be laid flat with long sweeping strokes of the body brush in the direction of the coat. At regular intervals throughout this grooming the body brush should be cleaned out on the curry comb, say every three or four strokes. From time to time the scurf and dirt should be knocked out of the curry comb on a hard surface – not in the stable where it can get back onto the horse or into the wind if grooming outside, but somewhere where it can eventually be swept away. On completion of the near side, the off side should be groomed in a similar fashion but with the body brush held in the left hand and the curry comb in the right.

Once the grooming of the body has been completed, the head, face and ears should be brushed carefully but thoroughly with the body brush.

The mane and tail can next be separated carefully with the fingers, never with either a brush or the mane and tail comb. Brushing and combing cause the hair to curl and eventually break, leaving both mane and tail sparse and untidy. Both, from time to time, will require to be pulled, preferably in either spring or autumn when the horse's coat is changing, or after exercise when the animal is warm. The hair should then come out more easily.

Pulling the mane and tail is done to give both a tidy but natural look. The clippers or scissors should never be used. When the mane has been carefully laid flat it can easily be seen which hairs should be pulled out to make it lie even and tidy. The length of the mane is a matter of choice and some breeds have their own particular rules. In general the mane is kept long enough to plait but short enough to be tidy. Starting with the longest hairs a few at a time are pulled from the underside of the mane. Four or five hairs are wrapped around the mane comb and pulled out with a sharp tug. This does not hurt the horse as he does not have a nerve ending at the hair root as humans do. It should be done with care as manes take a long time to grow and careless pulling may result in an untidy mane.

The hairs from either side of the root of the tail can be carefully pulled in the same manner to encourage the tail to lie neatly

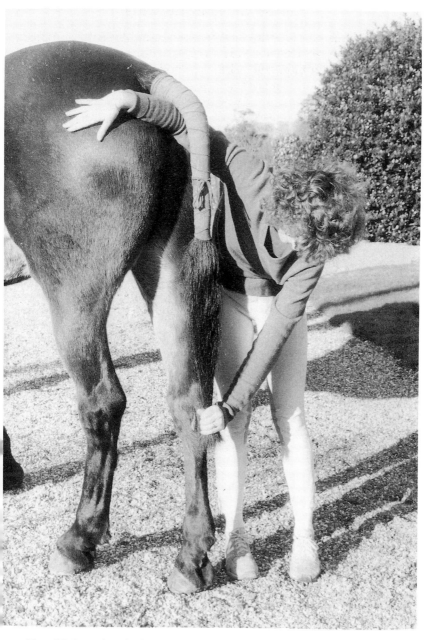

Plate 36 Assessing the length of the tail. With the tail raised it should be trimmed a hand's breadth below the point of the hock

between the points of the buttocks. Assessing the length of the tail is shown in Plate 36, and it can be finished as a 'switch' tail (in a point) or as a 'bang' tail (square) (see Figs 19 and 20).

On completion of grooming the tail should be bandaged for an hour or so, down to the end of the dock, and the mane can be laid flat with a damp water brush.

The eyes and nostrils can then be cleaned with one damp sponge, and the dock with another. Stallions and geldings require the sheath to be washed with mild soap and warm water about once a week. The 'squelching' sound sometimes heard when the male horse trots is a sign of a dirty sheath and neglect.

Washing the horse, in hot conditions, is refreshing and useful. He can be hosed down to remove dirt and sweat and the surplus

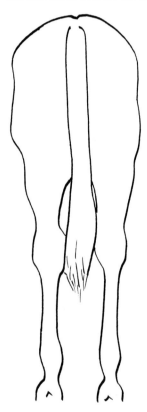

Fig 19 Switch tail

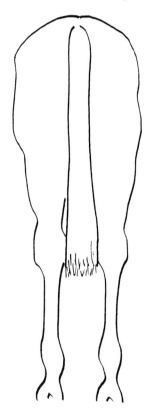

Fig 20 Bang tail

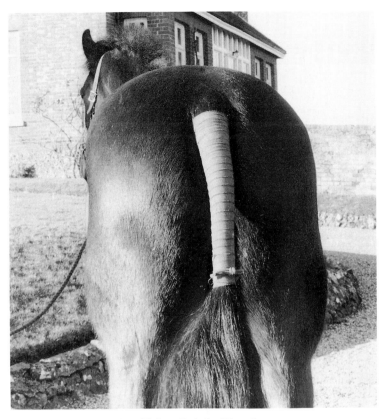

Plate 37 A well-tied tail bandage

water removed with a sweat scraper. He should then be walked quietly until he is dry. No part of the horse should ever be washed that cannot be thoroughly dried.

When a horse returns to the stable with his legs covered in wet mud, as he may after hunting, it is a mistake to wash them. It is better to wrap the legs, mud and all, in woollen bandages overnight, let them dry, and brush off the dry mud in the morning.

Strapping
Strapping is the banging of the muscular parts of the horse with a leather pad, a hay wisp, a stable rubber or the hand. It is done when grooming is complete and serves as a massage for the competition horse to tone up the muscles.

Quartering

Quartering is done first thing in the morning. It consists of removing the night stains from the horse's body with the dandy brush and the straw or shavings from his mane and tail with the hands, then picking out his feet and sponging his eyes, nose and dock. The rugs are not completely removed but folded back, first in front of the girth area and then behind.

Grooming the grass-kept horse

The grass-kept horse needs to have his feet picked out at least once a day. His mane and tail should be freed from mud and dirt daily and heavy mud and dirt should be removed from his legs and body with a dandy brush. It should be remembered that the natural oils and greases in the horse's coat help to keep him warm and protect him from the elements. When the grass-kept horse is required to hunt or compete, which requires fairly thorough grooming, some other form of protection must be provided as a substitute for the natural protection that has been removed. Certainly a New Zealand rug, a field shelter and extra feed will be necessary, together with facilities to bring him in at night should the weather become very cold.

Clipping

The horse's coat grows and is shed with the seasons of the year. It grows to its full length by the first part of the winter, is shed in the spring and is at its best by mid-summer. An early cold spell may encourage the coat to grow early and a warm early spring may cause the coat to be shed early. The growth and texture of the coat vary very much from breed to breed. Whilst well-bred animals in most breeds have silky coats, the mountain and moorland breeds tend to grow longer, thicker coats than the thoroughbred or the Arab.

The active riding horse, or competition horse, cannot be fully trained or worked without being clipped at some stage, or stages, throughout the year. The horse is clipped for four main reasons: to enable him to be worked hard; to enable him to dry off quickly after work; to facilitate grooming and keeping him clean and healthy; to improve appearance.

Electric clippers are now universally used, making clipping a task within the ability of most competent horse owners. When selecting a set of clippers, apart from the price, the following points should be considered:

1 How much work will they be required to do? Should they be heavy duty, capable of clipping many horses or will they be used for only one horse perhaps twice a year?
2 How heavy are they? Clipping horses is quite hard work and the weight of the clippers may be a consideration.
3 Do they get hot in use?
4 Are they easy to clean and maintain?
5 Are spare parts available?
6 Can the blades be resharpened?

There are many makes and various types of clipper on the market, from heavy duty to lightweight, battery-operated models. It is therefore worth making a thorough study of those available before deciding on which model to buy.

There are a number of accepted types of clip, and the one selected should be the one most suitable for the horse and the work in which he is engaged. The various types are shown in Fig 21.

Having decided upon the type of clip there are a number of preparations that must be made before clipping can start.

The horse should be clipped in a suitable, well-lit loose box on a dry floor. A thick rubber floor is an advantage but not often available. A competent assistant can be very helpful, particularly when the horse is difficult to clip. It is sensible for the person clipping the horse to wear overalls, a hat or head scarf and rubber-soled boots.

Spare blades should be readily at hand, together with a can of light machine oil and a small plastic dish of paraffin for cleaning off the blades from time to time. Needless to say, clipping should start with at least one, preferably two sets of new or newly sharpened blades available for use.

Consideration should be given to the extra rugs that the horse will require after his coat has been removed, and these should be readily at hand.

The most important aspect of all in preparation for clipping is that the horse should be thoroughly clean and dry. Clipping will almost certainly be difficult and uncomfortable if the horse has not been thoroughly groomed. He should be fitted with a head

Fig 21 The four most practical and acceptable types of clip (from top to bottom): hunter clip; blanket clip; chaser clip; trace clip

collar and loosely tied to a ring in the wall or held by an assistant. A hay net will help to keep him occupied.

The type of clip to be made can be marked out on the horse with chalk to help those who may not have an eye for a straight line. Tailor's chalk is useful for this purpose. Where a saddle patch is to be left, the numnah can be rested on the horse's back in the correct position and drawn round with chalk to help to get the correct size and shape of the patch.

Clipping should start at the neck and work towards the rear of the horse. The clippers are used in long strokes against the lie of the coat. It should not be necessary to apply pressure, the weight of the clippers is sufficient to achieve an even clip. The machine must be cleaned and oiled at regular intervals throughout the clip. If it gets hot clipping must stop while it cools down. Should the horse break into a sweat, work must stop, as it is not possible to clip a wet horse. If the blades become blunt they must be replaced and the tension carefully set with the adjuster screw to achieve the best results.

Horses that object to being clipped are usually distressed because the clippers are hot, blunt, or both, or they have not been introduced tactfully to the sound and feel of the clipping machine. If necessary a twitch can be used, but this should only be as a last resort.

The head, ears and other difficult parts should be left until last. The hair that protrudes from the ears can be trimmed level with the edge of the ear. Heels and fetlocks can be trimmed with scissors and a comb, but scissors must never be used on the mane or tail.

Some time at the end of September or the beginning of October the coat will begin to look dull and coarse. This is an indication that the winter coat is about to start growing. Hunters are usually required to look their best for the opening meet during the first week in November, so most owners will therefore delay the first full clip until the last week in October. This is a good time to clip as the winter coat will be well established. The horse may well have been given a 'chaser' or a 'trace' clip six to eight weeks before this to enable him to be got fit for the hunting season.

The coat will continue to grow during the winter and a second or even third clip may be required. The final clip should not be made after the end of January as this may well spoil the growth of the new spring coat. The rate of growth of the horse's coat will vary considerably between types of horse, and the climatic conditions will also have an effect. The decision on when and how to clip must be made bearing these factors in mind.

5 Saddlery and Equipment

Without a good quality, correctly fitting saddle and bridle the horse cannot be ridden correctly, comfortably or safely. The riding horse also requires other items of equipment which will be covered in this chapter.

Secondhand saddlery is often available at horse sales and at the saddler's shop. It can be an economy to buy used tack, but great care should be taken. Careful inspection should be made, particularly to the tree of a secondhand saddle as these are sometimes damaged beyond repair, and the condition of the leather, stitching, buckles and other fittings should be checked on other items.

The Saddle

Whilst it is important that the correct type of saddle should be used for a particular equestrian sport, it is more important, if only for the sake of the horse, that it should fit correctly. It is false economy to buy a cheap saddle; the best quality only should be used even at the risk of straining the budget. A saddle made from the best quality leather by a skilled craftsman, if properly looked after, will last a lifetime. Often the well-kept saddle will appreciate in value over the years. To buy and use a poor quality, cheap saddle will certainly prove uneconomical, may prove unsatisfactory or uncomfortable and, worst of all, cause injury to the horse.

Saddles fall broadly into four groups: dressage; jumping; general purpose; showing. There are other specialist saddles that are beyond the scope of this discussion.

The dressage saddle is shorter and deeper in the seat than the general purpose saddle, with a more upright head; the saddle flaps are cut straight and long; the stirrup bars are set more or less under the seat; the girth tabs are long and the girths short. It is designed to assist the rider to sit deep in the bottom of the saddle, with a long leg. The shape of the saddle and the set of the stirrup

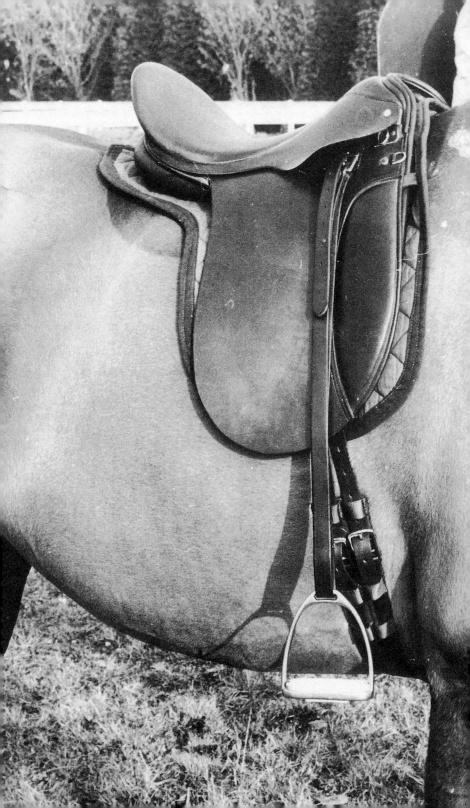

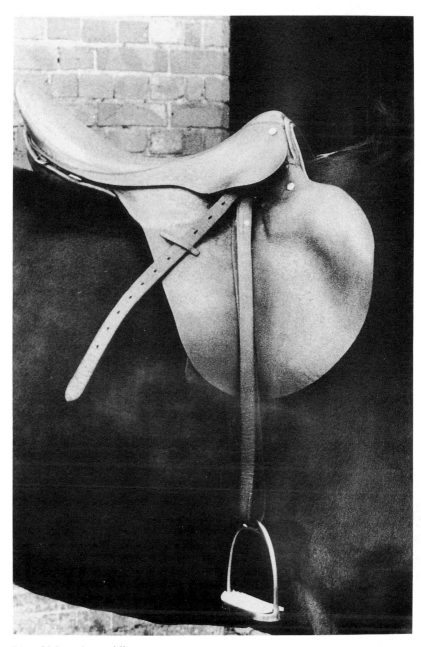

Plate 39 Jumping saddle

Plate 38 Dressage saddle

Plate 40 General purpose saddle

bars help with the maintenance of the most effective riding position. The long tabs and the short girths permit the rider's legs to be kept in close contact with the horse's sides.

The jumping saddle is made longer and more shallow in the seat; the flaps are cut forward with knee rolls and sometimes thigh rolls. It is usually built on a spring tree to relieve both horse and rider of some of the strain that might be put upon them in the rigours of jumping. The stirrup bars are set further forward to allow the rider to sit with a short stirrup and the knee bent. The knee and thigh rolls help to keep the leg position secure. The saddle is made longer to allow the rider the freedom of movement that is required when jumping and to adjust the position of the upper body.

The general purpose saddle is more like a jumping than a dressage saddle. It is usually built on a spring tree with the flaps cut slightly forward and a slight knee roll. It is ideal, as the name implies, for general purpose riding, and perfectly adequate for hunting, hacking and most jumping. It is not really suitable for dressage riding, even at the most modest level, as it does not encourage or allow the absolutely correct riding position which is fundamental in dressage.

The showing saddle is designed to show off the horse to his best possible advantage. It is often cut back at the head, the flaps are cut straight and long, and the stirrup bars are set to the rear. The purpose of this is to enable the saddle to be fitted further back, showing off the shoulder.

Saddles are measured in inches from the pommel to the cantle. Adult saddles range from about 15 to 18in. Where the saddle is cut back at the head the measurement is taken from the stud at the side of the head, to the cantle. It is important that the saddle fits both the horse and the rider. A reputable saddler will usually visit a stable and bring a selection of saddles in various sizes to try on a horse. He may even allow a customer to take two or three saddles on approval to select a suitable one. It is best, however, that it is fitted to the horse by an expert.

The saddle is designed to distribute the weight of the rider over the horse's back as evenly as possible. It must not touch the horse's spine at all. A clear channel must be left from the withers to the back of the saddle, only the padded panels coming in contact with the horse's lumbar muscles. These checks must of

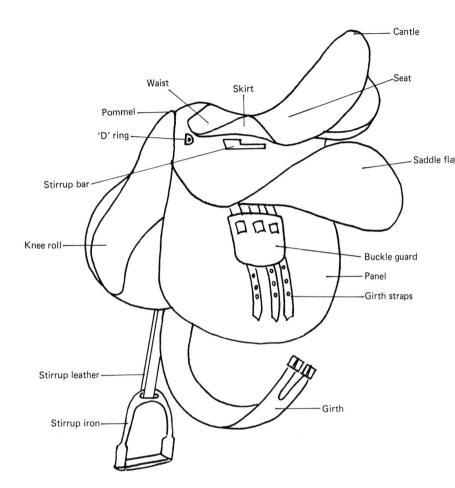

Fig 22 A general purpose saddle

course be made with the rider in the saddle.

Saddles are built on a wooden tree, usually beech. In some, the tree is sprung with a steel insert. In all cases the tree is fairly fragile and a fall, or a horse rolling on a saddle may damage it. Continued use of a saddle with a broken tree would almost certainly cause the horse discomfort and injury.

A new saddle requires the attention of the saddler after about six months' use. It needs to be checked and will probably require some more stuffing, the original stuffing having been compressed. Thereafter the saddle should be checked over by a saddler every year or so to ensure its continued reliable service.

The best stirrups are made in stainless steel, which is strong, safe and easy to keep clean. Nickel stirrup irons are weak and bend or crack easily. Ordinary steel stirrup irons tend to rust and are difficult to keep clean. It is important that stirrup irons are the right size for the rider's foot. If they are too large the foot may slip right through the iron and get caught. If they are too small the riding boot may become wedged in the iron.

Stirrup leathers must be safe and easy to adjust when the rider is mounted. Rawhide leathers are best, being very strong and durable, but they tend to stretch. Plain leather is quite satisfactory but the holes do wear and the leathers do eventually break. Stirrup leathers must be cleaned and saddle soaped regularly. Particular care must be given to wear on the buckle holes and stitching.

Girths are made in many different styles. They are found in nylon, leather and various types of string and webbing. Leather is the best material as it is safest, it lasts longer than the other materials and is easy to maintain in a soft, supple condition which is so important to the horse. Girths are made in various lengths from about 24 to 50in and must be the correct length for the horse. If they are too short they can be difficult to fit and adjust; too long and they may not be able to be fastened securely. It is a disadvantage to have the girth buckles too high up under the rider's legs as this tends to cause discomfort, and keeps the legs away from the horse's sides. Whichever type of girth is used it must be kept clean, supple and in a good state of repair.

The Bridle

There are two types of bridle that are acceptable to the serious rider: the simple snaffle bridle with a cavesson, dropped or crossed noseband, and the simple double bridle. There are other types of bridles and bits but discussion of them is not included here as they do not play a part in correct equitation. They are used, in general, to control a poorly-trained horse or by riders who have insufficient skill to ride correctly. At times they are used by very skilled riders who are taking a 'short cut' in the horse's training or who have insufficient time to retrain the horse.

The snaffle bridle is used for everyday work. There are many types of snaffle bit that are available but only a few of them are acceptable to the serious student of equitation. These are: the ordinary snaffle with jointed mouthpiece; the racing snaffle ('D' ring); the egg-butt snaffle, with or without cheeks; the Fulmer cheek snaffle; the wire-ring straight bar snaffle.

The cavesson noseband completes the bridle, but unless it is fitted quite tightly it has no practical effect. The dropped noseband, fitted correctly, discourages the horse from opening his mouth too wide or crossing his jaw. It is particularly effective and tidy when used with the Fulmer cheek snaffle bit. Care must be taken to ensure that the dropped noseband is fitted sufficiently high; it must not be fitted low, on the soft part of the nose. The dropped noseband must never be used with a bit that incorporates a curb chain. The 'flash' noseband has a similar effect to the dropped noseband. The 'grakle' or 'crossed' noseband applies pressure to the jaw above and below the bit. Its effect is, once again, to discourage the horse from opening his mouth too wide or from crossing his jaw.

When the horse can do all his work adequately in the snaffle he can be introduced to the double bridle. This bridle helps the horse to work at the highest levels of collection and with maximum impulsion. It gives the rider greater control of the horse, particularly giving him more influence over the lower jaw. It is not designed, nor should it be used, for the control of a horse so lacking in training that it would be difficult or dangerous to ride without it.

The correct fitting of any bridle is most important if it is to be both safe and effective.

Plate 41 Snaffle bridle with a cavesson noseband

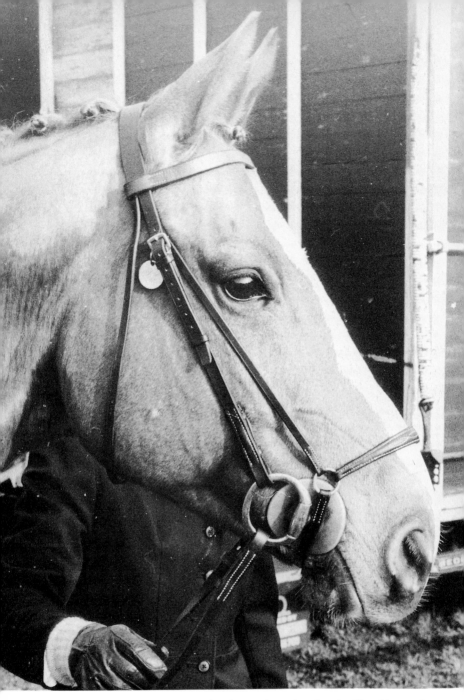

Plate 42 Snaffle bridle with a dropped noseband and rubber bit guards

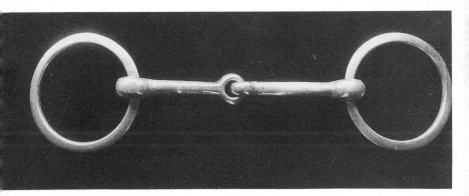

Plate 43 Flat-ring jointed snaffle

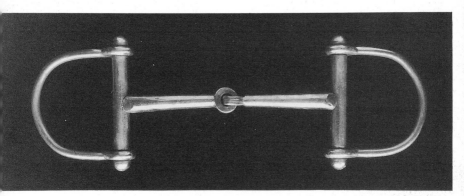

Plate 44 'D' ring snaffle

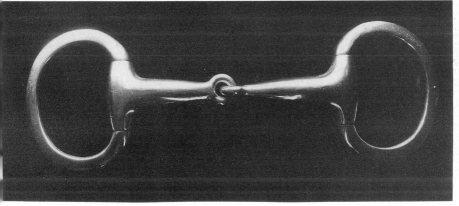

Plate 45 Jointed egg-butt snaffle

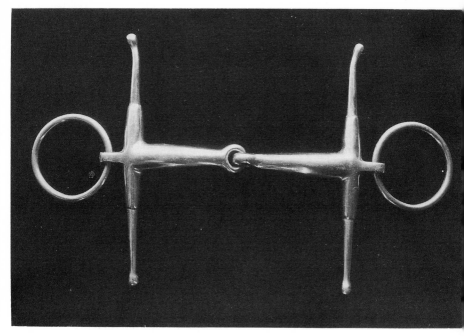

Plate 46 Fulmer cheek snaffle

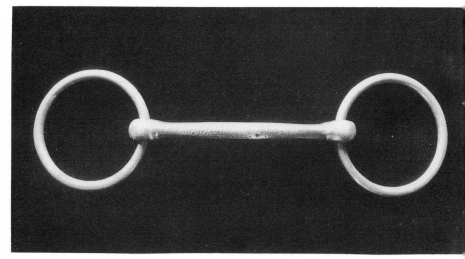

Plate 47 Wire-ring straight bar snaffle

Other Equipment

The numnah

This is a pad which is put under the saddle to provide some soft cushioning for the horse and to some extent to keep the leather lining of the saddle from coming into direct contact with the horse's back. The numnah must never be used in an attempt to make an ill-fitting saddle fit a horse.

Numnahs are made from various materials, the best being real sheepskin. These, when fitted with the woollen side towards the horse, provide good cushioning and allow a certain amount of air-flow between the saddle and the horse. Artificial sheepskins are available which have the added advantage of being easily washable. Perhaps the most popular numnah is made from nylon padded with foam rubber. Unless this is quite thick the amount of cushioning is minimal, but thick sponge rubber can upset the stability of the saddle. The nylon numnah is however inexpensive and easy to wash.

Whichever type is used it should be fastened securely to the saddle so that there is no possibility of its slipping out whilst the horse is being ridden.

Martingales

In some cases, due to bad training, conformation or temperament, the horse may when working raise his head above the level of control. Martingales are designed to prevent this from happening. The two acceptable and effective types are:

The running martingale, which works from the girth, between the forelegs, through a neck-strap onto the reins and bit, to the bars of the horse's mouth. It should not be adjusted so that the effect of the martingale is constantly applied, but should be of such a length that it comes into effect just before the horse raises his head to an unacceptable height (see Plate 48).

The standing martingale which works from the girth, between the forelegs and through a neckstrap to attach to the cavesson noseband. It must not be fitted to a noseband that goes below the bit. As with the running martingale, it should be adjusted so that it only comes into effect just before the horse raises his head to an unacceptable height. It must not be constantly in effect (see Plate 49).

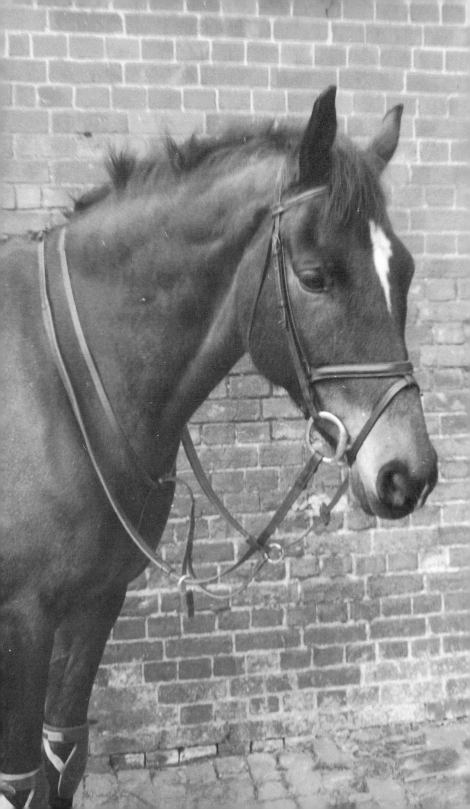

Plate 49 Standing martingale

Plate 48 Running martingale fitted with a flash noseband

Head collars

The stabled horse requires a head collar of either leather or nylon. Leather is easy to clean, strong and durable. It looks attractive but is expensive. Nylon is cheap, very strong (perhaps too strong), durable but unattractive to look at. The stable head collar should be fitted with a rope about 1.2 to 1.5m long (4 to 5ft), attached by a spring clip. Head collars are made in three standard sizes: pony, cob and full size. The cost varies depending on the standard of workmanship and the quality of the materials used.

Rugs

The horse requires a jute night rug and a lightweight rug to wear underneath it in cold weather. These are made in various lengths, measured in inches from the buckles on the breast to the rear edge. They come in various weights depending on the quality of the jute, the woollen lining and fittings.

Other rugs are available which are convenient but more costly. A multi-purpose rug is made in quilted nylon which is smart in appearance, machine-washable and serves as a day, night or travelling rug. A sweat rug, made on the string vest principle, is useful for drying off a hot, sweaty horse or for providing extra warmth under a day rug in cold conditions. It should not be left on at night as it may become damaged when the horse lies down. A cotton summer sheet is useful on a hot day to protect the horse from flies, dust and the sun. Coloured woollen day rugs are available and whilst they are very smart and practical they are very expensive. All rugs should be secured by a roller or surcingle and a fillet string.

The grass-kept horse requires, at certain times of the year, a New Zealand rug. This is a canvas, waterproof rug giving very good protection and is wool lined for added warmth. It has a secure surcingle and thigh straps which, when correctly fitted,

Plate 50 The Polywarm rug made of light, quilted nylon. It can be used as a day or night rug, or for travelling. It is machine-washable, which is a great advantage over jute rugs; the cross-over securing straps avoid the risk of pressure on the back so often encountered with the conventional roller; it also gives a very smart appearance

Plate 51 Woollen travelling or day rug

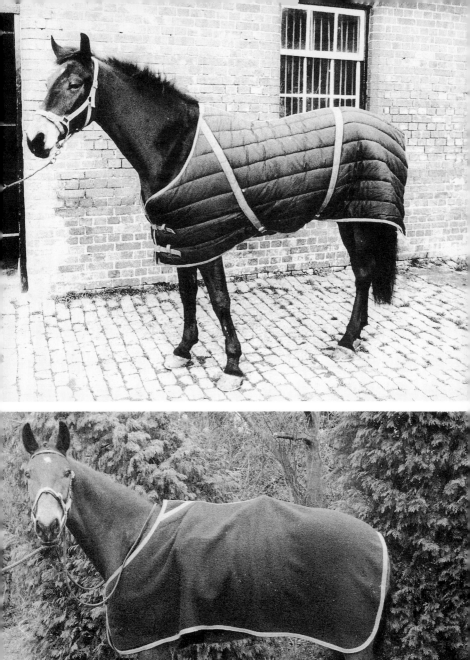

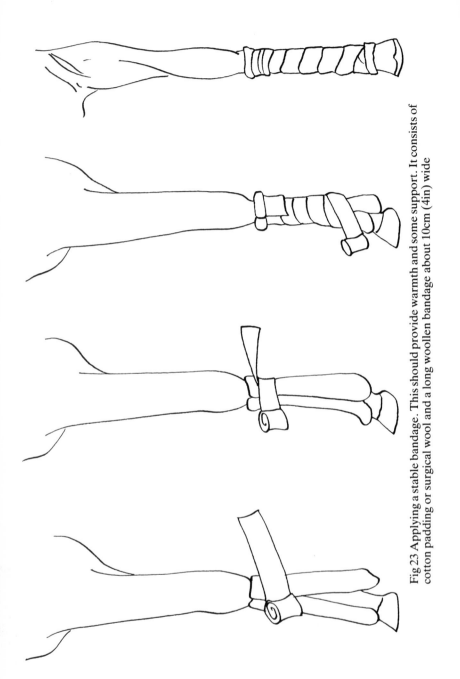

Fig 23 Applying a stable bandage. This should provide warmth and some support. It consists of cotton padding or surgical wool and a long woollen bandage about 10cm (4in) wide

ensure that the rug stays in position in all weathers and under most normal circumstances (see Plate 27).

Bandages and boots

A tail bandage and four woollen leg bandages are required, the leg bandages for warmth and support whilst in the stable and the tail bandage for keeping the tail neat and tidy. (The equipment needed for travelling is covered in Chapter 6.)

A variety of boots and bandages is available to protect the horse's legs when he is working. Exercise bandages are elasticated and about 1.2m (4ft) in length and 7cm (3in) wide. They are never applied directly to the legs but are fitted over cotton wool or gamgee. They must be very securely fastened with

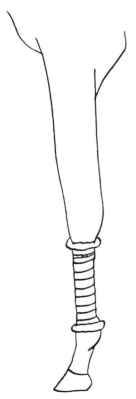

Fig 24 Exercise bandage. A 7·5cm (3in) cotton stretch bandage is used over gamgee or cotton wool. The bandage is secured with tapes which are usually stitched on

tied tapes, stitching or sticking plaster. This bandage is fitted from above the fetlock joint to just below the knee (Fig 24).

Exercise boots come in a variety of styles and materials. The best is the padded, leather brushing boot which is strong, durable and easy to keep clean and supple. A similar boot is available made in felt with a buckle or velcro fastening. These are cheaper but less robust than leather (Fig 25).

A useful and inexpensive boot is the over-reach or bell boot which is made of rubber and is pulled on over the foot to protect the bulbs of the heels on the forefeet (see Plate 52).

Care of Saddlery
This expensive equipment will give long service if it is carefully stored and maintained. All leather saddlery should be hung in a dry store when not in use. It very soon deteriorates if it is left in a

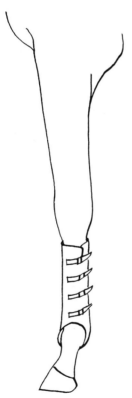

Fig 25 Leather brushing boot. There are usually four straps on the foreleg boot and five on the hind leg boot

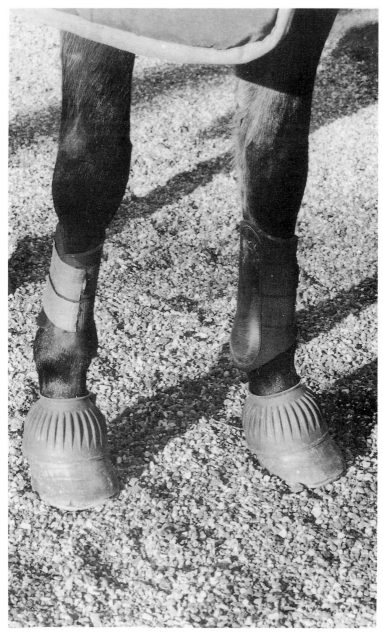

Plate 52 Felt brushing boots with a velcro fastening and over-reach or bell boots

damp environment or is not hung up correctly. The practice of putting saddles, or any leather equipment, on the ground almost always results in damage being caused.

The saddle, bridle and any other equipment used should be washed clean every day with a warm, damp cloth and treated with saddle soap. At least once a week the saddle and bridle should be taken apart, thoroughly washed, dried and saddle soaped. This treatment helps to prolong the life of the equipment and also ensures that the leather that comes in contact with the horse or the rider is kept soft and supple.

6 Transporting the Horse by Road

The ability to transport the horse by road is a necessity for any serious horse owner, but travelling arrangements can prove frustrating and disappointing if not carefully studied and considered. There are basically three ways in which the horse can be transported: by a horse transport contractor; in a trailer drawn behind a car; in a truck specially modified for the carriage of horses or livestock.

Horse Transport Contractor
This method may be suitable for the horse owner who only occasionally requires to transport his horse and for whom owning a box or trailer would be an extravagance. It may be useful for a family that perhaps has two or three ponies to travel from time to time, and does not have the facilities for keeping a box or a trailer.

This method can be expensive and inconvenient. Most contractors charge by the mile with a basic minimum charge, which, needless to say, should be agreed upon before any arrangements are made.

The Trailer
This is probably the most popular method. It is widely and successfully used by many amateur and semi-professional horse owners who have one or two horses or ponies to travel. It saves the encumbrance of owning, garaging and maintaining a box, and provides the mobility of a motor car once the trailer is parked.

Driving a motor car and towing a trailer is a tiring and exacting task. It may prove too demanding for some people if a long journey is to be undertaken, followed by a day's hunting or competing, and a long drive home.

The standard trailer is designed as either a single horse or double horse transporter. Some are designed to carry three or more animals but are comparatively rare in Britain. They are frequently found in the United States or Australia.

The trailer is built on a metal chassis with bodywork of either wood, metal or both. Those built in aluminium alloy are of course lighter in weight but may be less robust than those built in hard wood.

Access to the trailer is by a rear ramp and many are fitted with front ramps to allow the horse to be led out forwards on unloading. Those without front ramps are slightly less convenient as the horse has to be backed out.

Trailers designed to carry two horses are fitted with a central partition running from front to rear. These partitions are padded and are usually removable. The hard wood floor can be covered in thick rubber matting or some other washable, non-slip material. The trailer should be fitted with breast bars and breeching straps. A tie ring should be fitted for each horse which will probably also be used to hang a hay net.

Most trailers are now on a four-wheel chassis, two wheels having proved unsatisfactory for carrying any real load over a distance. A 'jockey' wheel is fitted to support the front of the trailer when it is detached from the towing vehicle. All trailers should carry a spare wheel.

Some trailers are fitted with an independent braking system, and some are without brakes, relying on the towing vehicle to stop them. Those without brakes must not, by law, exceed 750kg (15cwt) in total weight, ie trailer and load combined. The maximum gross weight must be painted on all unbraked trailers in a clearly visible position. It is an offence to load a trailer beyond its marked maximum gross weight.

The suspension of the trailer depends upon the load that it is designed to carry. It will usually be of the leaf spring type and may or may not include shock absorbers.

The trailer should be fitted with retractable stabiliser feet that can be lowered for loading and unloading but *must*, together with the jockey wheel, be raised before moving off.

There are many extras that can be provided with a trailer to prolong its life and to make it easier to use, for example, an interior light, a saddle rack, water carrier, spare wheel lock, auto-reverse mechanism, rust proofing, underseal etc.

Like any other vehicle that is to remain efficient and reliable,

Plate 53 The stabiliser feet in good order

Plate 54 The stabiliser feet bent and misused

Plate 55 The towing hitch must be in good condition, free from excessive wear on the ratchet pawl, springs, levers, clips and other moving parts

the trailer must be maintained regularly. Tyres are very important and must be kept at the manufacturer's recommended pressures. Wheel bearings, break linkages, suspension, towing gear, hinges and latches all require regular, correct lubrication if they are to remain trouble free. The stabiliser feet and jockey wheel can be particular problems if their retaining wing nuts and moving parts are not kept lubricated. Prompt removal of rust patches, rust proofing and repainting are all essential items of maintenance that are often overlooked.

The variety of trailers available is very wide. Some are sold as being suitable to be towed by a motor car with an engine as small as 1300cc. For sustained hard wear, however, and one's peace of mind, 2000cc, and preferably four-wheel drive, would be an advantage when towing any loaded trailer off a muddy show ground. The law requires that the towing vehicle is at least twice the weight of the loaded trailer. On roads other than restricted roads and motorways, towing vehicles which have an unladen weight of not more than 1.5 tons have a maximum permitted speed of 50 miles per hour. This is sometimes reduced to 40 miles per hour. The towing vehicle registration number must, by law, be displayed on the back of the trailer.

New trailers, purchased from reputable dealers, carry a warranty on parts and labour for a limited period, but buying a secondhand trailer can be more hazardous. One's first impressions of cleanliness and freedom from superficial damage and rust are important. A trailer that has clearly been looked after externally may well be in good condition mechanically. Re-sprayed or newly painted bodywork may arouse suspicion; certainly a potential buyer should ask why it has been repainted.

The balance of the trailer should be good, the sides should not bulge when viewed from the rear and there should be no lean on either the bodywork or the wheels. The tyres should have a good depth of tread over the entire surface and show no signs of uneven wear. Uneven tyre wear may be a sign of many other faults that may be expensive to rectify.

The towing hitch must be in good condition, free from excessive wear on the ratchet pawl, springs, levers, clips and other moving parts. The jockey wheel and stabiliser feet must be unbent and move freely. The braking system must move freely and show no signs of wear. The ramps and doors must fit well and be easy to open and close. The internal padding, including that on the partition, should be sound. The partition must be easy to move and adjust. Above all, the woodwork of the floor must be sound and free from rot.

The trailer should be fitted with rear lights, brake lights, reflectors and traffic indicators. These are operated by a connecting plug which attaches to the towing vehicle.

When buying a trailer the potential purchaser should take it on a test run using the vehicle that he intends to drive when transporting his horses. It is an advantage on this run to test the trailer with horses in it. Special attention should be paid to the balance of the loaded trailer, with particular reference to the effect that it has on the towing vehicle.

The height of the towing hook on the vehicle is critical. Most towing hooks can be adjusted for height and if in doubt professional advice should be sought. A safety chain is fitted to the trailer to ensure that it remains attached to the towing vehicle should the towing hook fail. Care must be taken to ensure that this can be fitted satisfactorily.

On the test run the brakes must be tested, remembering that the trailer, and its load, will make the braking effect of the towing vehicle less efficient than normal. An assistant will be required to check that the rear lights, brake lights and trafficators are all in working order.

Reversing a trailer does not come easily to all drivers; it requires practice. Some trailers require a reversing catch to be lowered in the braking system before they can be reversed, and this should be checked on the test run.

As a guide to assessing the weight of the load that a trailer will be required to carry, a 12.2 hands pony will weigh about 250 to 300kg (5 to 6cwt), a cob or similar riding horse at 15 hands about 400 to 460kg (8 to 9cwt) and a heavyweight hunter about 500 to 600kg (10 to 12cwt).

The Horse Box
The truck, or horse box, is the favoured method of those who travel a lot and cover long distances carrying five or six horses. It is easier driving than towing a trailer, makes a less tiring journey for the horses, can provide accommodation for grooms and riders, and storage space for tack and feed.

The ownership of a horse box involves tying up a good deal of capital in the vehicle and the necessity of finding somewhere to park it. Running costs are high, but may of course be offset where the vehicle can also be used as a farm vehicle or for other commerical transport tasks.

A wide range of horse boxes is manufactured to provide for those who require to move one or two horses in comfort on a regular basis, right up to those who are continually on the move, over long periods of time, with eight or nine horses.

At the top end of the range are vehicles over 7.5 tons laden weight. The drivers of these vehicles must hold Heavy Goods Vehicles drivers' licences and the vehicles must be fitted with a tachograph. Obtaining an HGV licence is a demanding and expensive task. To stand a reasonable chance of passing the test it is necessary to attend a professionally run course, the fees for which are currently some hundreds of pounds. The fee for taking the test is also high, and should a candidate fail he or she is required to pay the full fee again at any subsequent sitting of the test.

The vehicles are very expensive but they do provide every modern convenience for both the horses and their attendants. They can be fitted with sleeping accommodation for up to six people, a kitchen, all toilet facilities, running hot water, refrigerator, television etc.

Maintenance costs are also high, including fuel, insurance, repairs and servicing. This must however be put against the cost of hotel bills and the other inconveniences of staff being accommodated away from their horses.

It is not, however, necessary to go to these lengths with a horse box. A two-horse box of less than 3.5 tons laden weight can be driven by a person over seventeen years of age who holds a licence to drive a car. This vehicle requires no tachograph.

Horse boxes that have an unladen weight of 1,525kg (30cwt) or more must be inspected annually at a Department of Transport vehicle testing station. This inspection includes a test of the brakes, chassis, steering and other important areas of the vehicle. It is known as 'plating' because a plate is issued showing the weight of the vehicle together with individual permitted axle weights. This plate must be fitted to the vehicle, usually to the inside of the passenger door.

Horse boxes are usually built on a standard vehicle chassis with the coachwork designed by a specialist horse box builder. They are constructed usually of wood or aluminium alloy, or a combination of the two. Petrol or diesel models are available. The cabs are often very comfortable and, apart from the overall size of the vehicle, driving them usually presents no difficulties to the average, competent motor car driver.

Preparing the Horse for a Journey
To ensure a safe journey it is necessary to take certain precautions. Most horses travel very well and are unaffected by the experience, others are clearly worried by travelling in a vehicle.

To protect the horse from physical injury whilst being transported he should be fitted with woollen travelling bandages or boots. These should cover the legs from the top of the cannon bone down to well over the coronet. They should provide both physical protection from blows to the legs, and warmth. Both knee and hock boots should be fitted. The tail should be bandaged and a tail guard fitted over the top of the bandage. Many tails have been spoilt by rubbing, even for only a short period, on the ramp of a trailer. A 'poll guard' can be fitted to the head collar to protect the poll should the horse throw up his head.

Depending on the climate, the horse may, or may not, need to wear rugs. On a cold day he may need a sweat rug and one or two woollen rugs. A journey in a horse box or trailer can be draughty and cold even when the air temperature is quite high on a sunny day. On a warm day it may only be necessary for the horse to wear a summer sheet to keep off the dust.

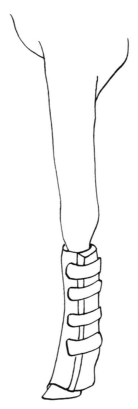

Fig 26 Travelling boot. Usually made from leather or plastic and padded with sponge rubber. The fasteners are velcro

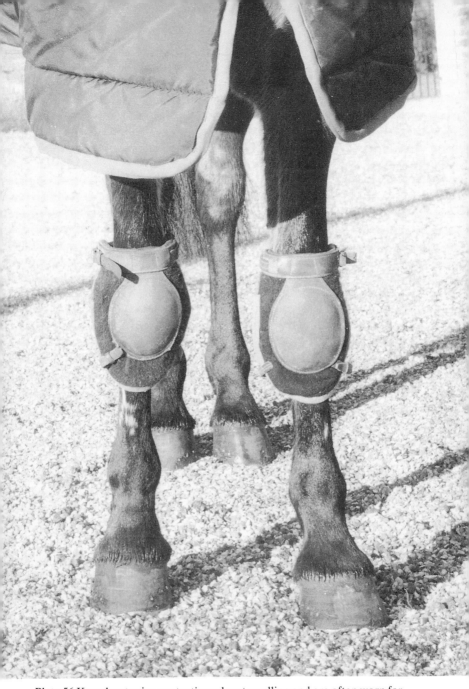

Plate 56 Knee boots give protection when travelling and are often worn for road work when a stumble could damage the knees

Plate 57 Sensibly dressed for travelling

A hay net usually keeps him occupied on a long journey. There are occasions when it is undesirable for a horse to have a large hay net prior to arrival and under these circumstances a small hay net is all that is necessary. When two horses are to travel together, a hay net each may discourage them from nipping at one another around the partition. If this does not work, then an extension board can be fitted to the front of the partition to keep their heads apart.

Some bad travellers have been known to travel more happily facing the rear. Some horses travel better alone, in a double horse trailer with the partition removed, so that they can stand at an angle, giving them a better chance to balance themselves. These variations are worth trying where a horse clearly has travelling difficulties.

Horses that are Difficult to Load

The horse that has been properly handled and trained since he was a foal should present no problems when being loaded into a horse box or trailer. He will have been transported, as a foal, with his mother and will have complete confidence in his handler. If, however, these elementary precautions were not taken at an early stage, and he was first bullied into a trailer at four or five years, and given a rough ride, it will almost certainly follow that the horse will be unwilling to load quietly. Further bullying, whipping and shouting will only compound the problem and he will be all the more reluctant next time.

Often horses refuse to enter the box because they have suffered traumatic experiences whilst travelling. A bad driver can put a horse off travelling and consequently make him difficult to load, with all the trouble and frustration that that can cause. The road speed should be kept down in order that the horse is given the smoothest possible ride. Coarse steering, braking, gear changing and accelerating are all contributory causes to making horses bad travellers. It is a strain for a horse to travel in a box or a trailer. The effects of claustrophobia and the generation of static electricity in the trailer can cause him discomfort. This combined with driving in 'fits and starts', can ensure that the horse will be difficult to load on future occasions.

Horses that are difficult to load should be taken to a quiet place, away from onlookers and other volunteering 'experts'. The fewer people that there are assisting the handler the better. The trailer should be parked close to a wall to discourage the horse from stepping off the ramp to one side. It is vital that the stabiliser feet on the trailer are lowered securely when the horse is being led in. Many a horse has been put to fright by a ramp that springs up and down when he puts his foot on it.

In a two-horse trailer the partition should be removed or taken well to one side. If two horses are to travel in one trailer it is often best to load the difficult one first, as he will have more room in the trailer to walk into.

The horse should be fitted with a lunge cavesson with a lunge rein attached to the centre ring. A stable head collar and a lead rope are not good for leading a horse that is reluctant to go into a trailer. It often helps if some straw is spread on the floor of the trailer and up the ramp. The handler should then, with the rein

Plate 58 A well-trained, willing loader

about 30 to 45cm (12 to 18in) long, walk up the ramp into the trailer leading the horse, the front door having been previously opened so that the horse can see straight through. The handler can leave by the front door. He must look straight to his front, not backwards at the horse. He can take in his hand a few oats or horse cubes to encourage the horse, and to reward him if he leads on well. The assistant should stand on the open side of the trailer with the horse between him and the wall. He should be ready to encourage the horse forward by a click of the tongue or a slap on the quarters.

With the really reluctant loader it sometimes helps to fit the lunge cavesson as described above, and to pass the lunge rein through the ring in the front of the trailer and back out of the trailer past the horse. It should not, of course, be used with great force but the tension should be carefully taken up to encourage the horse to walk forward without the encumbrance of the handler standing in the trailer in front of him.

Racehorses that are reluctant to enter the starting stalls are often almost carried in by the loaders, who link arms just below the buttocks and above the hamstrings to lift them forwards. This method can be used to get a horse into a trailer but it is potentially dangerous and should be left to those who are skilled at it. The racehorse, after all, has only to stand in the starting stalls for a few seconds. The horse being loaded into a trailer may be there for some time.

Loading into a vehicle is part of the horse's basic training. It should not be left until a few minutes before departure for a show or the opening meet. The best possible method of persuading a difficult horse to load is to allow him to find his own way in. If possible he should be put in a very bare paddock with little grass and no water. The trailer is then put in the paddock with the brakes on and the stabiliser feet down. The ramp is lowered and the horse's feed and water are put in the trailer up at the far end so that he has to walk right inside to reach them. It is usually not long before he is walking in and out of the trailer quite calmly of his own accord.

Index